THANK YOU FOR MY CHILDREN

THANK YOU FOR MY CHILDREN

A High School Teacher's Final-Year Journal, Anecdotes and Observations

Jason,
I hope your S.H.S years were as good for you as can be, and that the future is even better!
Rick Pepe

Rick Pepe

While the incidents in this book did happen, some of the names and personal characteristics of some of the individuals have been changed. Any resulting resemblance to persons living or dead is entirely coincidental and unintentional.

Thank You for My Children:
A High School Teacher's Final-Year Journal, Anecdotes and Observations

Cover design by Melissa Mykal Batalin
Book design by Jessika Hazelton
Author photo by Dan Pepe • hitchphoto.com

Printed in the United States of America

The Troy Book Makers • Troy, New York • thetroybookmakers.com

To order additional copies of this title,
contact your favorite local bookstore
or visit www.tbmbooks.com

ISBN: 978-1-61468-0437

DEDICATION

For Elisa, whose idea this journal was.
Your love and support sustain and inspire me.

For Dad, whose love of a good story
first showed me how to "work a room".

For Mom, whose love of books
first set me on my life's path.

For Christina and Dan,
the children I'm most thankful for,
who are now on that same path.
May you enjoy it as much as I have.

I hope I've made you all proud.

Special thanks to friends and colleagues, old and new,
and especially to Jim LaBate and Jay DeTraglia
for valuable suggestions and advice.
Indians or Saints, we are all One.

Contents

February

March

April

May

June

Foreword

This book is far too brief to be a career-long "highlight film", and far too informal to be a "do-it-this-way" manual for beginners. It is hardly about pedagogy at all. Rather, it is a final-year journal kept in the hope that it might clarify for those who know me just exactly why I enjoyed the work so much, and perhaps give others who might read it some insight not into how to teach, but into how to enjoy it, and to enjoy learning from it. I have learned a great deal about teaching, most of it from my students; this is my chance to pass some of it along. At the suggestion of trusted friends, I've added anecdotes spanning my entire career and observations about those journal entries and anecdotes.

You may recognize the main title as a line of dialogue spoken by Atticus Finch in Harper Lee's *To Kill a Mockingbird.* It encapsulates my feelings not only for my own children whose mom, my life's greatest blessing, I met in Schalmont's halls, but for the forty-five hundred students I've had the pleasure to teach, coach, and advise. They are, in a sense, my children too.

Miss Lee once said in a rare interview that *Mockingbird* is "a love story". I wondered for quite a while why she would describe a book with no romance in that way. Now, having written one, I finally understand what she meant.

Princetown, New York
July 2011

Introduction

The realization that I wanted to be a high school teacher first hit me in the tenth grade. I don't remember the actual moment of epiphany; it crept up on me. I'd known from Day One that I liked school, because I was good at it. Don't we usually enjoy the things we're good at?

Early on, a "good report card" was routine for me and took little effort. This lasted until high school when the work got harder and my effort, largely underdeveloped, didn't keep pace. An "A" student all through grade school (even skipping third grade, to graduate at sixteen), I kept a solid "B" average through high school. My work ethic finally caught up to my academic ability in college, from which I graduated with a Dean's List G.P.A..

One thing was certain all the way through my pre-college years: if I enjoyed a subject, I did well in it. As a prolific reader with a good memory, it isn't surprising that I enjoyed English and history most of all. I'd always enjoyed a good story, and those classes were where I encountered the best ones. Today, I have an M.A. in English Education and thirty-three credits toward a Social Studies teaching certificate. My love of stories, fictional or real, is why I chose to pursue credentials in these areas, but it is not why I chose to teach in the first place.

Ask me how I knew at age fourteen that teaching high school would be perfect for me, and I'll answer with a shrug. I just *knew,* but not from any particular personal experience. My parents were not teachers, nor were my aunts or uncles. I had no neighbors who taught, nor any adult friends. The majority of teachers in my K-12 parochial school were nuns, whose only conversations with us about vocations were centered on the religious life. They were dedicated, hardworking women who were caring, fair, sometimes brilliant teachers, most of whom didn't appear to be having much fun doing it. (Maybe that was our fault.) I can't recall any of them discussing teaching as a career with us as a class, and certainly not with me as an individual. No, there were no adults in my life who tried to "sell me" on the value and virtue of a teaching career. Thankfully, neither were there any who tried to steer me away from it.

The idea that I should try to do a little good in the world while I'm here – probably first planted by those good Sisters of St. Joseph and later nurtured by my exposure to the "Franciscan tradition" at Siena College – in an honorable and even noble profession, one in which I felt I could be successful and happy, seemed worth pursuing.

There are, of course, many careers where one can "do good in the world", but how many of them also allow you to spend your working hours (and so many after-hours) with kids? "Doing a little good" – or a lot – for kids?

At age fourteen, I wanted a career that I could enjoy. That was paramount. I thought little about honor and nobility, and not at all about salary. It has never been about money (a good thing, since my first year's wage was about $7800. I still couldn't quote my exact final year salary; it just doesn't matter that much to me). I wanted to make a difference and have fun doing it. A life spent among high school kids seemed to be the way to go.

Boy, was I right.

September

"If you make children happy now, you will make them happy twenty years hence, by the memory of it."

- Kate Douglas Wiggin

Behind the mike – Fall '07 Pep Rally

September Lesson

Monday, 9/1/08

Labor Day: no work. (What a country!) But tomorrow marks the beginning of the end of my teaching career. Year 37, ready for lift-off. Looking forward to it… as always.

Today I discovered a *Star Trek-TNG* marathon on the SciFi Channel and settled in for a while. First up (for me, anyway): "Relics", the episode wherein the *Enterprise* crew find a crashed vessel whose transporter, locked in an endless loop, contains the biopattern of Capt. Montgomery Scott, the original series' "Scotty", who had figured out that putting himself into the transporter indefinitely was necessary to save his life and give himself a shot at eventual rescue as his own ship's life-support systems began to fail. Now, seventy-five years later, he is brought back, meets the new crew, tours their new, modern *Enterprise,* and quickly comes to realize that, his skills mostly outdated, he may well have outlived his usefulness. That's a feeling I hope to avoid in this, my last go-round teaching high school English.

Capt. Picard, understanding Scotty's dilemma, instructs his crew to try to make him feel useful, wisely noting that that is a basic need of every person – to feel useful.

So far I still feel useful, even as the end of my career looms nearer than ever. Still, I find it ironic to catch that episode again at this point in time. Of course, Scotty's vast knowledge of how things used to be done in his day saves the new *Enterprise* from a major disaster in the end, and he leaves for a new life in a retirement colony having made a huge difference in the present, just as he always had in the past.

God, I love that episode.

Tuesday, 9/2/08 – "Staff Development", Day 1. Irony abounds! In 1972, my first year here, on our first staff day in September, new teachers were taken on a trip by school bus to view the various far-flung elementary schools in our district. No such trip was made in any year since until today, when all district teachers were taken to SUNY Albany's College of Nanotech Science to learn a bit about this new technology. Again, we went *via school bus.* That's two opening-day bus trips in thirty-seven years on the job, one in my first year, the other in my last. None in between. Sort of appropriate in a symbolic way; a long career of high school teaching book-ended by two trips in a school bus.

It didn't get any more comfortable, but the company was better.

Wednesday, 9/3/08 – "Staff Development", Day 2. First English Department meeting of the year, and the first seen through the eyes of a prospective retiree. We are all different, all professional, all memorable in our own ways. I'm proud to be a teacher, more proud to be an English teacher, and prouder still to be in this group, with these people. Not to mention those who've left us (willingly or otherwise) whom I've looked up to through the years. I wonder if these colleagues look up to me.

Tomorrow the kids come back. Can't wait! Empty school halls are the saddest places, I think. After all this time I feel no fear, no butterflies, just curiosity. Will they allow me to enjoy my last go-round? We'll see.

It was a bit less than wonderful today. My class assignments were nothing like I'd requested, my schedule (classes and planning periods) different from what I've grown very comfortable with lately, my class rosters sprinkled with kids I'd rather not have back for another try, my lunch at a time when I'm not hungry yet, except for the camaraderie of old friends which I won't be sharing, their lunch period not having changed.

Some of these things can't be changed, some can (guidance has promised to try to move the repeaters if possible). None of these are things I haven't dealt with before – just not all at once. I suppose I'll just suck it up, take one for the team, learn to live with it. I guess it could happen to anyone, even one with thirty-six years of service and much seniority. Anyway, it'll make a good cautionary tale for young teachers in the future, should any care to listen.

I blame it on the scheduling software, which could care less.

Thursday, 9/4/08 – The kids have arrived! The halls are happy again and so am I, the schedule be damned. I'm reminded yet again why I do this...it's the best job in the world. For me, *children* and *laughter* are the two most beautiful words in the language. Nothing lets them bloom like a school, and I'm happy to help the process along. Speaking of blooms, I was presented with a gift of potted flowers by Mary, my next-door neighbor of nearly twenty years, along with her best wishes for a great final year at Schalmont. A heartfelt gesture from a long-time friend.

Only a few colleagues know of my retirement plan. I think I'll let it leak out at whatever pace it will. To announce it at a meeting or some general faculty gathering would seem like fishing for some sort of tribute, like a retiring NBA star making his last swing through opponents' arenas. In a place where everyone knows everyone else's business in short order, it won't remain a secret for long.

I suppose I ought to confide it to my principal, though.

Friday, 9/5/08 – Day 2 of lunch alone. For some reason (probably computers) I'm stuck in first lunch, earlier than the one I've enjoyed for many years. I don't *need* to eat at 10:45; apparently no one else does either. Every faculty member who has the choice of when to take lunch (unlike me) must be choosing to do so later, or maybe eating in their rooms. In my final year I must forgo the spirit-boost that comes from colleagues' stories, jokes, advice…just from their company. The only advantage to this that I can see so far is that with fewer people around the office area, the more likely it is that the copy machine will be available – and with no opportunity except this lonely lunchtime to use it between 8:30 and 1:30, that's really quite fortunate.

Look for the silver lining, I guess.

Tuesday, 9/9/08 – It's becoming clear that not every day of this final year will be noteworthy. I hope I'll know it when they are – and not just in retrospect.

Our Student Council advisor asked today if I'd once again M.C. the annual Homecoming Pep Rally. Of course

I said yes, I'd be delighted. It's set for Friday the 26th. I wonder if the principal will again introduce me as "the Voice of Schalmont." It's corny and a bit embarrassing after all these years, but I secretly love it.

Especially now.

Friday, 9/12/08 – Another season begun, announcing the home football games from the press box for the spectators, identifying ball carriers and their tacklers, playing tunes for cheerleader routines, pushing concession-stand snacks and whatever else I'm asked to say. This season I've been asked to break in a student announcer, a senior who aspires to a career in sports journalism and eventually, broadcasting. Of course I'll do it, and happily; our task of preparing kids for their futures isn't, and shouldn't be, confined to the classroom.

9:30 PM: Gino, our intern, did a great job in his debut, and he's going to get better.

Monday, 9/15/08 – Saw a girl in the hall today whom I'd taught in English 9 and 10. She semi-seriously asked, "Why can't you teach English 11?" I explained that the schedule works better with me at 9th and 10th, that nothing could be done to change it at this point, and that the teachers at that level have more experience with that curriculum than I do. As she hurried away to her next class she said over her shoulder, "Maybe you can teach 12th next year?" I thought, but couldn't say, I won't be here next year. Too soon, too soon.

Later, I typed up a vocab quiz and brought it to the copier to make class sets to use in a few days' time. As is my custom, when I returned to class I stashed the original copy in my file cabinet for use *next year.* Old habits die hard, and some probably never.

And there will only be more of them sneaking up on me as the year unfolds.

Friday, 9/19/08 – The second home football game of the season: an upset victory over a traditionally superior rival. Gino has improved significantly in only one week, so much so that I could leave the press box for a bit to grab a snack at the concession. Ironically, I wound up in a conversation with his parents, dad being a former student of ours. As we talked, several other alumni drifted by, some joining the chat. None could believe how much time had passed since they themselves were students here, some as long as thirty years before. As I had been on staff before they'd even entered as freshmen, talk turned to questions about my future plans, and how much longer I might stay.

Though I deflected those questions as tactfully and as unspecifically as I could, I got a sense that my leaving would close a chapter in their lives, too; when there are still some of your old teachers doing their professional thing in the same place you remember, the door to your youth remains open, if just a crack.

I think I'll keep coming back to these games as often as I can. Though my own students will no longer be on the field or on the court, for a good many years to come they and their parents, many also once my students, will be on the sidelines, in the bleachers, or working the concession. If I can still be their link to a simpler, more carefree time in their lives, it's the least I can do.

I owe them that much, and more.

Friday, 9/26/08 – Big day today: the Homecoming Pep Rally, followed by various afternoon sporting events and culminating in the Homecoming football game. I'll be the M.C. for the rally (my last) and the announcer for the game, possibly my last unless the team is awarded a post-season playoff game at home.

2:30 PM: Well, the weather drove us into the gym for the rally, but it went well. Easy, really – just welcome everyone to the event, announce the Homecoming events to follow, introduce the coaches and finally, keep talking till the dismissal bell rings, in case we run short! Fortunately, the timing was great; the bell rang as I finished up my final reminders. The kids piled down the bleachers, the faculty drifted away, the teams went off to prepare for battle and there I stood, microphone still in hand, finally having enough down time to grapple with the realization that I will never get to do this again – a service I have rendered most every year since the 1970s. I've known this day was coming for some time but the creeping reality, as I stood in the now-empty gym, set me to wondering: who'll do this next year?

Earlier, before he handed me the microphone, our Athletic Director introduced me as "the Voice of Schalmont." Pretty cool, I think, after all. But whose voice will it be next year?

For the kids' sake, I hope it's at least an enthusiastic one.

9:30 PM: What a great Homecoming game! A 39 to 0 victory, a margin pretty rare in these parts, and against a competitive opponent, too. The team didn't want to leave the field.

Two things stood out for me though, besides calling the Big Win. The first was announcing the presentation of his jersey to the family of a popular player who was killed about four months ago in a road accident. Without doubt the saddest thing I've ever had to speak into a microphone. Minutes later, one of the most delightful things I've done: holding the mike in the press box as our award-winning concert choir sang the National Anthem. It may be one of the highlights of my announcing career, surrounded by a semi-circle of great singers as they poured their hearts and voices into the microphone that I held in their midst.

Truthfully, if the anthem is performed well and my mood is receptive, I'll sometimes tear up, regardless of the time and place. This was a struggle for me tonight. I could not make it to the end of the song without nearly losing it. Realizing that eye contact would unravel me, I just closed my eyes and gave them a big smile. Inside, I was a mess. What a treat on my (possibly) last night working a game. I tried to hold that mike as steady as I could so as not to tip them off with a trembling hand. I'm not sure I was successful.

September 1972

New Class Advisor

Our college education professors had suggested that we'd better be ready to deal with all sorts of emotions that we'd experience in our early days on the job – nervousness, confusion, worry. They never mentioned one I'd never anticipated: TERROR.

I'd been in front of my classes for a grand total of three days when the word came from the office that the four class advisors would meet with their classes the next day "to prepare for election of officers and to begin planning this year's activities." I knew this day was coming since I'd agreed to be freshman class advisor on the August day I was interviewed.

Those same college profs had advised us not to get involved with clubs, coaching and extracurriculars until we'd been teaching for a year or so. Teaching is tough enough when you're new, without those other "outside" activities to dilute your focus, they'd said, which seemed reasonable at the time.

Just the same, while sitting in that interview room being grilled by the principal, English department chairman, and assistant superintendent of schools, my professors' advice on that particular subject didn't seem so very reasonable at all. Not with God knows how many other job applicants and interviews they had to consider. Eventually, the question came.

"Would you consider taking on the job of freshman class advisor, if hired?" I nodded eagerly and said, "Yes, of course, I think I'd enjoy doing that."

What else could I say if I hoped to get the job? I could not have known how true those words would turn out to be.

But my first encounter with the class was anything but auspicious. Our meeting had been scheduled on one-half of the gymnasium, with the sophomore meeting to take place simultaneously on the other side of the partition wall. I waited by the door with the vice-principal as the frosh piled in, to sit in the bleachers and wait for the show to start. Knowing that I and I alone was the show didn't help my nerves any. Knowing that kindly and well-liked Mr. Morrison, the vice-principal, had my back did.

But not for long. After asking for quiet and getting it, Mr. Morrison introduced me. I can't remember if, after sizing me up, they clapped. (*I* wouldn't have.) Though I had some prepared items to discuss, I was a wreck. Three things made this a much greater challenge for a brand-new teacher than it should have been.

First, after introducing me, kindly Mr. Morrison walked out the door and into the lobby and vanished. So much for administrative backup.

Second, there was not one other teacher on our side of the gym besides me. I was on my own with two hundred twenty freshmen. Things would change in the years to come; the administration would eventually require all teachers who bring their classes to an assembly to remain with them for crowd control. But that was still several years in the future. On that day in 1972, all the freshman teachers had dumped their classes in the gym and fled, probably to have a good laugh with Mr. Morrison somewhere.

Third, the layout of our gym was not conducive to a presentation of this type. Our bleachers consisted of eight rows of seats the length of the basketball court along both sidelines. Because the gym had been divided in half for these class meetings, the two hundred twenty freshmen had to squeeze themselves into two sets of these low-rise bleachers on either side of the court. Half of them on each side, impossible to keep them all in sight at once, with me in the middle of the floor alternately shouting at and pleading with either side to please listen, this is important class business that you need to hear.

Oh, and one more thing: no one had thought to provide any sort of voice amplification. Just me and two hundred twenty squirming fourteen-year-olds in two clumps fifty feet apart requiring me, the twenty-two year-old newbie, to turn my back to half of them at any point and shout so as to be heard by all. I remember thinking that, if I got anything useful accomplished at this meeting, facing classes capped at thirty would be cake.

Somehow, some useful things were accomplished that day. I asked for nominations for officers – good people who'd work hard for the class, no gag-nominations please – and got several. Those who were elected the following week did a great job; most remained officers for the entire four years. Some still serve as reunion-leaders to this day.

I grew as a teacher that day, though I didn't realize it until later. I learned not to be afraid of large numbers of teenagers, even if you don't know them yet. I learned that a teacher's youth can be an asset rather than a handicap, and that the veterans don't have all the answers. And I learned the importance of bonding with your students on some level so they can see that, though the "big desk" sometimes comes between us, we all want basically the same things – to matter, to be respected, to make a difference.

Sometimes I'm asked how that bond between myself and the Class of '76 was established, how our happy relationship of thirty-eight-years-and-counting took off. I believe it started on that very first day when, during a rare moment of quiet in that noisy gym, I said, "Listen, I'm new here and you're new here. Neither of us knows what's going on yet. Neither of us is sure of what to do. We have a lot to learn. I think it'll be better for all of us if we learn it together."

In my desperation to fill up the allotted time for the meeting, I'd let my guard down and tried to appeal to their better nature, to assure them that, though a rookie, they could count on me to be their advocate, that I would "have their backs" to whatever extent my nearly negligible faculty status would permit. Thankfully, it made as much sense to them as it did to me. We were off and running – together – and still are.

September Observation

Forget all that advice about "not smiling till Christmas", or January, or whatever arbitrary date your particular early mentors (college professors, internship hosts) suggest.

That might be a good idea while interning, but once you land a position of your own, be real. Be accessible, emotionally as well as after school. Be yourself – it's your classroom, after all.

Certainly, even a humorless drudge of a teacher can be successful in raising student achievement by respecting and valuing his kids, by acknowledging them and treating them with fairness. No argument there. I have also found that letting yourself be seen as a real person with a life outside school and interesting personal stories who likes to laugh and have reasonable fun with students pays big dividends in the classroom and beyond, outside of class and for years to come. Few teacher-trainers would argue with that. Many would, however, disagree with my suggestion to "show your real self" right from the start, as I did. They'd prefer you wait till later in the year when you have a "handle" (whatever that means) on your kids. I believed that realness and humor was how you *got* that handle. My first English Department chairman disagreed, in writing, after an observation during my first year.

"Mr. Pepe has potential, but will only get the most from it if he spends more time on lesson planning than on extracurricular activities," he wrote. He knew that I was extremely involved in my class advisor duties, chaperoning school events, and attending as many athletic events as I could (I was not yet coaching). I was determined to immerse myself as much as possible in the life of the school, to enjoy this new experience as fully as I could. I believed that being a "real person" would earn me the respect and trust of my students in a way that my shaky classroom management skills could not yet do. But my department chair thought my focus needed some shifting, so I took his advice and, without cutting back on school activities, spent more time on careful lesson planning.

Apparently, he became pleased with my growth; subsequent class observations seemed more to his liking. They were generally more complimentary, and his end-of-year evaluation in June of my third year – the one that could make or break my getting tenure – was memorable for its positive tone and for its irony. He was pleased to recommend my continued employment, and commended me for my "special rapport with his students" and "valuable presence in the school community," or words to that effect.

I was exhilarated. I would be getting tenure, and I'd made progress in my teaching while maintaining my busy schedule of school activities (now even busier with the addition of varsity softball coaching). Perhaps I'd made progress in my teaching *because* I'd maintained – even increased – my schedule of activities, and perhaps not. I like to think so. And I like having done it my way, without sacrificing those things that gave me so much joy.

Be real. Tell your stories. Get involved. Smile. Laugh. It worked for me!

October

"Remember, son, you must always use your powers for good."

- Pa Kent

DJ - Homecoming Dance '78
(Check out the vinyl.)

October Lesson

Thursday, 10/2/08

Open House for parents, aka "Back to School Night". This is a very accurate label in our district. So many of our parents are also alumni, which isn't strange at all in a small community such as this. It's amusing, and perhaps amazing, to watch your former students file in and head for the same parts of the classroom that they preferred in their own student days. This time, there will be no re-ordering of seats alphabetically to better learn their names. I already know most of them, share memories with them and, in some cases, remember *their* parents in this same setting so long ago.

I marvel at the resemblance some of my students have to their parents: the same type hair, the same posture, the same walk, vocal timbre, tilt of the head when listening, the same facial expressions. When I have taught or coached *both* parents, the effect is even more powerful. Sometimes I struggle not to call a boy by his dad's name, or a girl by her mom's. I must be especially careful about this when the parent has predeceased us; not a common occurrence, thankfully, but a good one to be aware of beforehand. I have two such students this year in the same class.

Whether their parents were once my students, my athletes or my class or club officers, these kids have history in their eyes. My history.

Wednesday, 10/8/08 – My first Athletic Association meeting of the year. I like to attend when I can to offer my input, to ask for funding for an unbudgeted softball program need, or just to be an unofficial liaison to the staff and other coaches. This evening, as the previous meeting's minutes were read, I glanced around at the parents in attendance. There were eight, all of whom I either knew well or had at least met. Of the eight, I'd taught half. Of the eight's eighteen children who'd come through our school, I'd taught eleven.

I imagine there are teachers who wouldn't care to be a member of a parent-dominated organization, who'd never consider living in the district where they work, or who wouldn't think of having their own kids attend those schools. For us, it's the best thing we could've done, a personal choice that has helped us in the classroom, created lasting friendships (some with former students-turned-parents), given us a more credible voice in district affairs, and possibly enhanced parents' attitudes toward our staff in general. Who knows?

But first you have to stick around for awhile.

Friday, 10/24/08 – Today Elisa and I, together with eight other English Department colleagues, attended the annual New York State English Council Conference in Albany. I thought I still might pick up some ideas or strategies I might use, however close to the end I might be. And I did! Still, it was a bit surreal having lunch with hundreds of New York State's finest and knowing it probably will be the last time for me.

At one point I found myself chatting with a former student, a former student-teacher, and a young former colleague now working elsewhere – all at the same time! (I considered scanning the room for one of my own former English teachers but didn't bother, figuring that they're probably all dead.) To be the link, the bridge to a time and place that helped shape their life stories and gave some direction to their careers was at once exhilarating and sobering. What a gift, what a privilege, what a responsibility this profession is – all at the same time.

During the final luncheon the Council recognizes "Educators of Excellence" from around the state who have "inspired excellence in students as well as teachers." Normally I just applaud them – they deserve it – and wonder what they've done to receive this award. It's sort of like being the high school senior who never did much for four years watching his more driven classmates being called up on stage by the principal on Senior Awards Night to collect their scholarships. Oh well, one last time won't hurt, I thought. But a surprise awaited me.

The incoming Council president, our master of ceremonies, announced the final award winners, then said he had one more person to recognize...and called my name, asking me to stand. What on earth for? I wondered. He then proceeded to tell this elite (compared to me, anyway) gathering that I'd be retiring at the end of the year after thirty-seven years of service, without having taken a single sick day. "I'd like to know your secret," he added.

It figures. At a function honoring the creative and innovative, I get recognized for longevity, stamina and good genes. (Could be worse...could be posthumous.) Of course Elisa (the true innovator in the family) put him up to this using her connections as a presenter at previous conferences. Afterward she told me that my "achievement" needed to be recognized by a group much larger than just our own school faculty, which would happen anyway in due time at year's end. Even better was his mention that "their daughter Christina is a previous winner of the statewide NYSEC student scholarship" for a student pursuing a career as a secondary ELA teacher. Though her achievement rather than mine, it gives me greater satisfaction.

Though the ripple of "ooh" and "wow" from the luncheon crowd upon hearing the "no sick days" comment was gratifying, and though I suppose not many have equaled it, to me it's no big deal. When your employer is paying you whether you show up for work or not (we are allowed fifteen sick days per year), showing up is a matter of pride and honor. It's what you're supposed to do unless you're highly contagious or at death's door. For me, it's about good health (a gift from God), the good example of parents who rarely took a day off, and the love of a good woman to bring it all into focus.

And I've got the best. Thanks again, Lord.

Tonight we have a playoff football game on our home field. One more announcing gig for me. A good thing; I wasn't ready for it to end.

Wednesday, 10/29 – As it turns out, Friday's game wasn't the end of the line, for the team or for me. Their record, the best since the 1960's, has earned them another game tonight. Win or lose, it will be the last; no possibility of going to the Dome in Syracuse for the state championship exists, despite their success. One last announcing gig. It should be fun – but still more fun if we win.

10:00 PM: It's over. The season, the fun of announcing, all of it. Naturally, as far as your humble announcer was concerned, the evening was more "beautiful," the good plays on the field more "exciting," the food at the concession more "delicious" than ever before. (I suppose the announcing was a bit more "corny" than previously too, but that's for the fans to decide. So far, no complaints.) The game was a blowout win for us, 39 to 6. Everyone went home happy, on our side at least, including me. Too many good things happening around me to dwell for long on the finality of it all. I hope all of the "last things" go just as well, and end as happily.

October 1978:

Hottest Band in the School

Students have asked for my help both in and outside of the classroom many times through the years, but the most memorable – and fun – was in 1978 when four senior boys asked me to prepare them for what they hoped would be a Halloween Dance that people would remember for years: a guest appearance by the then "hottest band in the land" – KISS.

They had already begun working on their costumes, which turned out to be astonishingly accurate replicas of the band's regalia. There was Jeff, whose tightly-curled Italian 'fro made him the obvious choice for Paul Stanley; Jacques, the tallest, who would dye his blond locks to become Gene Simmons; George, whose lean physique and feathered hair gave the group its Ace Frehley; and Mike, whose shorter, sturdier frame fit Peter Criss to a "T".

They'd gotten photos from magazines (*Circus*? *Hit Parader*?) on which to base their costumes, but they would not be content, they told me, to strut around the gym, posing for snapshots with their "fans." Oh no, they wanted to perform, to give a mini-concert of perhaps two KISS songs. Only then would the strutting and posing begin.

I thought it was a great idea, with one crucial flaw: not one of them could play the requisite instrument. Undaunted by this, they filled me in on the plan: they would get real instruments and fake it for all they were worth, lip-synching the lyrics as they did. As a teenager in the 60's, I knew this could work. Didn't the pros do it every week on *Shindig, Hullabaloo* and *Bandstand?* I assumed they had sought me out because I was the usual DJ for school dances, so they could tell me what songs they wanted to fake, work on their introduction, and other such details. That was part of it, but they had a special request.

"We know you've seen KISS live before, right?"

I had, in fact. Three times by that point.

"Would you show us how they move, what each one does with his instrument, how they dance around the stage? You know all that stuff, right?"

I did. Many hours of air-guitar in my bachelor apartment had burned it into my muscle memory. But school was definitely not the place. Not that it was such an unseemly thing to do, but if anyone saw us it would ruin the surprise on dance night.

Not long thereafter we convened at my apartment where I schooled them one by one on each member's signature moves. We chose the songs and I played them as the guys studied my attempts to mimic Paul's high-stepping footwork, Gene's ominous bat-winged looming pose at the edge of the stage, and Ace's arched back, fretboard pointed up into space, all with my $39.95 cheapo Sears guitar. Mike was pretty much on his own; he could fake it behind the drum kit – or on my sofa pillows, this being rehearsal – well enough without much input from me.

What made all this work the night of the dance were their costumes (really phenomenal), their instruments (really professional), and the timing. They entered the gym balcony where they had set up to perform from a rear door and after all the paying customers were inside.

No one saw them enter the building until they were set to go. From my DJ perch far to the side of the upstairs gym, I leaned into the mike and gave my best take on the band's actual intro: "Ladies and gentlemen…would you please welcome…the hottest band in the land…KISS!!"

I dropped the needle into the groove, faded in on the opening power riff of "Rock and Roll All Nite" and sat back to watch the show. There are a lot of details about that performance that I'll never forget, but the most impressive for me were the faces of the dancers-turned-spectators, mouths agape, on the gym floor below us. I remain convinced that many of them, for a little while at least, believed that somehow the dance sponsors had gotten KISS to appear at our little Halloween event. In any case, nobody knew who was under that makeup and those costumes until the guys chose to lay down their weapons of sonic destruction after "Calling Dr. Love" and go downstairs to mingle.

I don't remember whether the guys won the traditional "Best Costume" prize or not. I certainly hope so; no one's ever put more work into it. I do know that they have matured into fine adults with significant lives and one very big, happy Halloween memory.

And KISS, of course, became "the hottest band in the *world*".

October Observation

In the spring of 1984, after living the bachelor life for nine years and the married-living-in-an-apartment life for nearly three years, Elisa and I decided it was time to buy a house. But where? We wanted out of our urban-apartment neighborhood, preferably to somewhere our children would have "room to roam" without necessarily leaving their own property.

We also didn't want a long commute to and from school each day, nor a long drive to campus to deliver our kids to and from the school activities we hoped (actually *knew*) they'd be joining in the future, wherever that school happened to be. So we began taking drives around the county on weekends in search of properties for sale that we found both appealing and convenient.

We found one we liked, priced to sell with plenty of acreage near major roads, and a quick commute to school – two miles, door-to-door. It met all of our requirements, but raised one major question: would it be advisable to live in the school district where we both worked, and where our children would attend school? At a distance of only two miles, we could count on both being the case.

We didn't agonize over our decision to buy the house, nor did we wait until we'd surveyed the few co-workers who'd lived in the district for years. Some of them had no children, others had sent theirs to private schools. Very few were in our situation, both living where they taught *and* sending their kids there as well. We found out only later that those few had experienced no real problems. We had to move on the property or risk losing it. That, and the allure of a five-minute commute, drove our decision to buy.

Overall, it was a great choice for us. The downsides were few: two or three episodes of "mailbox baseball" welcoming us to the neighborhood, and the occasional ear-bending at a little league or rec soccer game from a taxpayer with an axe to grind about proposed school tax hikes or teacher contract negotiations, and who knew a captive listener when she saw one. That's it. Not a big price to pay for decades of two-mile, five-minute commutes for two teachers and their kids, who were eventually involved in band, student government and a total of five interscholastic sports, with all the chauffeuring that entails.

To anyone contemplating setting up a home in the district where you teach, I say follow your heart but don't rule it out purely on the basis of hearsay, or fear of what *might* go wrong. It's possible your naysaying colleagues are at least partly to blame for their problems with the community. Consider instead what might go right; if you're the kind of teacher and neighbor you should be, it will. Working shoulder-to-shoulder with other residents, especially on school projects or events, builds great good will for you *and* for your teaching colleagues.

And there's no better way to get to know the kids (and families) your own children will want to hang out with!

*****

Just a few words about attending conferences, if I may: DO IT! Do it as often as you can spare the time and as the school budget (or your wallet) can spare the expense.

If you're starting out in teaching, it's the best way to stockpile ideas and materials which you still sorely need. If you're a veteran teacher, it's the best way to reinvigorate yourself, to remind you what you loved about your job in the first place.

No less an authority than Harry K. Wong, in his landmark book *The First Days of School,* advises us of the biggest secret to teaching success: Beg, Borrow, and Steal!

"It's really research and learning," says Wong. "You walk into the classrooms of effective teachers, look around, and if you see something that you think might help you, say, "Gimme, gimme, gimme!" At conferences, these effective teachers bring the best of their classrooms to you.

When you attend a conference in your field, you are stealing (with their permission) from a broader range of experienced professionals than can be found in your school alone. They will be effective practitioners, or they wouldn't selected as presenters of their particular specialty. And we *all* need what they have to say, "newbies" to build their inventories, "vets" to jump-start their possibly idling mojo.

All your life you've heard it's wrong to steal. Where teaching is concerned, it isn't wrong...it's Wong! And it's so right.

November

"The hidden curriculum is the teacher's own integrity and lived convictions. It is the lesson which endures a lifetime."

-Jonathan Kozol

Team bonding with the teacher-coach.

November Lesson

Wednesday, 11/5/08

This afternoon I took my final turn as a volunteer on the National Honor Society selection committee. I had done it several times in past years, recusing myself when my own daughter and son were candidates (they both made it). This is one service I will not miss next year. So much is riding on our decision to admit or not to admit these candidates, whose applications are always anonymous to us. And nothing brought that home to me so well as having had my own kids held up for scrutiny. Sure, the criteria are clear; it's not our fault if an applicant has not shown sufficient character, service or leadership (the scholarship criterion is met by all or they would not come up for consideration). Still, to vote "no" on this or that application is not something done lightly, or in haste, or without some agonizing on my part. However clear the criteria, however lacking one's achievement in a particular category may be – this is somebody's kid, one with plans not unlike our own long-ago dreams, whose chosen future might be put on hold by our decision here today, who might have to settle for a "Plan B" future or a second-choice college.

I've felt for a long time that being a parent makes you a more understanding (if not "better") coach, allowing you to see where a player or a parent with a problem is coming from. You suddenly see both sides of an issue with greater clarity, and empathy, than before. Of course this goes for teaching as well, in all its aspects. However difficult or deficient students may be, they are someone's most precious possessions. "They send us the best they have; they're not keeping the good ones home", a wise colleague once told me. Once this sinks in, committee work of this sort becomes much tougher.

I am glad to have served, but just as glad never to do it again.

Thursday, 11/20 – This evening I attended what may prove to be the last Drama Club performance I'll see while on staff: Kaufman and Hart's *You Can't Take It With You.*

Great title for a possible last-time experience. The irony is not lost on me.

I attended because I've always liked these student plays, and because the leading lady is a student in my period seven class. She did a great job! Having seen the play before in this same auditorium about thirty years before, I expected it to be amusing, and to be entertained. Both turned out to be the case. But this time the wise ruminations of Grandpa Vanderhof on the subject of his retirement, and on what really matters once age gives you the perspective to be able to reflect on your career, really nailed me right between the eyes:

How many of us would be willing to settle when we're young for what we eventually get? All those plans we make...what happens to them? It's only a handful of the lucky ones that can look back and say that they even came close.

I went to a play to be amused and entertained and came away feeling that Kaufman and Hart were speaking to me across the decades, in my own students' voices. Grandpa Vanderhof's take on career fulfillment confirmed what I've been feeling lately: that my early plans turned out very well indeed, that what I eventually got was better than I'd hoped for, and that I am one of those very lucky ones who not only came close but whose satisfaction exceeded his expectations.

So "You Can't Take It With You," huh? We'll see about that.

November 1995

Missed Chances

When you love your job and give some thought to why you came to love it or how it happened that you chose it to begin with, often the names and faces of those who served as your role models will swim into focus.

For me there were several, two of whom were especially influential in showing me the path I would myself take, and I let them both down. Maybe not technically, but certainly I could have done better by both of them. I didn't, and now I regret it.

Mrs. Laura Going taught me English in ninth and tenth grade, and made it enjoyable. It's safe to say that hers was my favorite class throughout all of high school. I couldn't have known then that I'd spend thirty-seven years teaching English 9 and 10 in various combinations. All I knew was that at a time when teaching was beginning to loom large as a career possibility, said enjoyment likely tipped the scales in favor of high school English. Today that enjoyment lingers in memory, though most of the lesson content has fled.

Whatever else I may have forgotten, I still smile to think of the chance she gave the "Big Four" – Walt, Jay,

Tom and I – to star in a classroom production as four of Shakespeare's most memorable: Brutus, Caesar, Antony, and Cassius, to our delight and the probable indifference of the rest of the class. I suppose she could tell how much I'd enjoyed that, just as I suppose she had heard much later that I'd become an English teacher, too. Mrs. G likely never knew that her example, as much as my aptitude for language or anything else, was the reason I'd followed in her footsteps. Now, as I knelt before her casket, it gnawed at me that I'd never taken the time to make the effort to tell her that, though I'd been teaching for twenty-three years at the time of her passing.

Kindergarten was an even longer time ago for me, but its lasting message (to me, anyway) – School is good! It can be fun! I can do this! – was imprinted on me by Sister Eileen Lomasney (aka Sister Mary Ada, CSJ) in 1955. Of course, being just a first-grader when Sister left our school in 1956, I lost track of her quickly and, I thought, permanently. I only occasionally wondered where and how she might be.

Many years later as I browsed the diocesan newspaper, I discovered an article about Sister, who had re-taken her birth name and had become rather well-known in her order and even beyond for her religious-themed poetry. Though she likely wouldn't remember me after so many years, wouldn't it be nice to get in touch again to thank her for making my initial school experience so positive that it helped illuminate my own career path years later? I had to do this!

If you've been paying attention you've guessed by now that I did nothing of the sort. As with Mrs. Going, I just put it off again and again until, just a few years later in that same diocesan newspaper, I happened upon Sister's obituary. I learned of her passing too late even to attend her services. Perhaps that's just as well; hers was yet another casket before which I felt unworthy to kneel. Once was enough.

We're all told endlessly in the media, from pulpits and by folks we know, to tell the people we love that we *do* love them, and what they've meant to us, before they're gone and it's too late. My corollary to that is this: whatever your career path, seek out those who've had the most to do with your choice, your direction, your successes and tell them, preferably in person, what role they played in all of that. And thank them, especially the teachers, who devoted their lives to shaping yours. Just keep in mind what I had to learn the hard way: THE TEACHER IN THE BOX CAN'T HEAR YOU.

November Observation

I've mentioned that becoming a parent makes you a more understanding (if not better) coach, able to see both sides of an issue with greater clarity, and empathy, than before. This goes for teaching as well; parenting gives the teacher a better understanding of what students' parents may say or do. You may not agree with them, but you'll understand where they're coming from.

This raises the issue of teachers coaching interscholastic sports, which I generally endorse, having done so for fifty-two seasons. Obviously, not every non-teacher who excelled at a sport can or should be attempting to teach it to students. Conversely, no teacher, no matter how effective a communicator, ought to be coaching a sport of which he or she has no knowledge simply because he *is* a teacher. But the teacher-coach does have certain advantages over the outsider-coach, in my opinion.

First and foremost is his presence in the school building – all day, every day. He will know easily which players were absent, and therefore not entitled to play or practice that day (and some will try anyway). She will know of any players whose misbehavior-based suspension has disqualified her from participation, and she'll know it instantly rather than when she arrives at school from her "other job", so she'll more promptly be able to adjust her lineup or practice plan for the day. He will be known by and easily accessible to his players' teachers, so he can stay informed of their academic progress and even take steps to motivate the athletes to hustle academically so they are allowed to hustle on the field or court.

It should be obvious that I have approached my coaching career as, among other things, a tool to be used to teach student-athletes good citizenship, academic effort, fair play, loyalty, teamwork and the importance of conducting themselves with class, any one of which alone is more important than won-loss records, personal stats, or possible athletic scholarships. Not that these three things have to be at odds with the previous six. Not at all. But in my experience, a teacher-coach is more likely to make the character- enhancing goals more of a priority. It's why we're there.

December

"Being a professional means doing your job on the days you don't feel like doing it."

- David Halberstam

PEPE'S FINAL TOUR
2009

37 Years of Teaching
6,800 Teaching Days
33,300 Total Classes
Over 345 Softball Coaching Wins
Over 950 Total Games Coached
1986 Section II Class B Girls Basketball Coach Year
Over 5,000 Miles Traveled to Away Games
Class Advisor for Class of 1976
Student Council Advisor from 1977 to 1998
Coach for "Answers Please" TV Quiz Show Team
The Voice of Schalmont Football
Boys Basketball Clock Operator
4 Time Winner of Who's Who Among America's Teachers
1 Girls Basketball Sectional Championship
2 Softball Championships
6 Girls Basketball Colonial Council Championships
Colonial Council (league) and Sectional (II)Championships in 2 Sports in the same year (1986)
Taught with 6 different Principals and Superintendents
Vinyl Record Guru

"The Man, The Myth, The Legend"

Unlike The Who, I only had one farewell tour.

December Lesson

Friday, 12/5/08

A tough week. The last time I'll ever teach my favorite book, *To Kill a Mockingbird.* The first time was in 1972, in my rookie year. I've taught it in twenty-five of my thirty-seven years, with close to 100 classes of sophomores. I tell Elisa that when I'm in my casket, along with my rosary beads I want a softball and a copy of *Mockingbird* in there with me. She thinks I'm kidding.

Of all the things, all the books I've shared with students, this will be the toughest to let go of. Of course I have a copy of the book, and the VHS and DVD versions of the film at home; I can read and see it any time. Nothing will compare to sharing it with kids who at first wrestle with its language, its regionalisms, its story set so firmly in the 1930's (which may as well be the 1530's as far as they are concerned), who then gradually realize that it has sneaked up on them, charmed them unlike any other schoolbook, and left them with life lessons that will take time to process and years to appreciate.

I think my presentation has communicated to them my joy at being the one to introduce them to it. I hope so. I told them today that I feel it is a privilege to have done so.

I know I choked up just a little as I closed the book for the last time on Monday, and teared up just a bit as the film faded to black today. I hid both well.

The joy to be found spending time explaining the nuances of something you love to kids who are willing to listen and learn is perhaps not easy for those who've never done so to fully appreciate. For me, few things compare.

Friday, 12/12 – My last Christmas party as a faculty member. A pleasant if rather small crowd, due to today being a snow day. Some would-be party-goers decided not to risk a trip to the restaurant via slippery roads. Elisa and I, being much closer, were the first ones to show.

Karen, a Schalmont teacher and graduate who organized the party, sat and chatted with us. Elisa told her how on the previous evening, Karen's son (currently one of Elisa's seventh-graders) came to his Christmas concert dressed as required except for the obligatory necktie, which he'd forgotten. Panicked, he sought Elisa's advice before the show. She went and got him one of the extra "emergency" ties the band director keeps handy and gave it to him. He looked at her and said, "But I can't tie this!" A high school senior boy assisting with the middle school concert quickly fixed him up, and all was well.

After telling Karen all this, Elisa said to her, "Bob (his dad) should show him how to tie a tie."

Karen replied, "Are you kidding? When we went to the Junior Prom, Rick had to tie Bob's tie, remember? I'm not sure he knows how, even now."

Hearing this story, I recalled for the first time in years that I had indeed helped Bob get his necktie right on the night of their prom, which Elisa and I had chaperoned. Though I'd completely forgotten that, Karen hadn't.

How many other things that I've done or said in three dozen years of interacting with students do they remember, sometimes for years and years? Things that I've said in passing, or in jest? Little, seemingly inconsequential things I've done not realizing that it might be a much bigger deal to the student who's watching or listening? And why did it take me so long to realize that this goes on?

Lord, please let the good ones outweigh the bad.

December 1972

The First Was the Worst

For the Four Seasons, a night in late December 1963 was worth commemorating in song. For me, an evening nine years later was significant in a much-less-pleasant-to-recall way. If I had to choose a song to immortalize it, "HELP!" would do nicely. But help was hard to come by at the time. Oh what a night, indeed.

One of the best pieces of advice I'd gotten in my first year of teaching, and one that I've passed on many times since, is to get as involved in extracurriculars as your personal and professional life allows. This came from my first principal, Mr. Corrigan, who indicated that since fluctuations in enrollment are inevitable, staffing cuts are sometimes necessary with the lowest in seniority the first to be trimmed. Since four new English teachers had come aboard that fall, one of us likely would be on the chopping block eventually.

"You want to make yourself as valuable as you can in as many ways as you can," he advised. "Give me a reason to keep you around if we have to make cuts."

This seemed like a good idea, coming from the man who'd have a lot to say about who might stay and who might go. I had already taken on the role of freshman class advisor. Since there were no teams in need of a coach yet, I'd get my name and face out there the only other way I could see – by chaperoning. Chaperoning every possible event, dance, ballgame, bus trip, anything where teacher presence was desirable.

As a twenty-two year-old with no wife, kids or property responsibilities, there was no reason not to. Which is how I wound up the sole teacher chaperone on the basketball spectator bus bound for Albany Academy in late December of my rookie year, 1972.

It was my first such trip, though the season had been underway for about a month. My biggest worry this night was whether the seniors and juniors would respect me as an authority figure since I'd never taught them. Some probably didn't even know my name.

Armed with the sign-up sheet and my still-emerging "teacher voice," I got them on board, took attendance and we were off to Albany. It was about a half-hour trip, but it would seem much longer.

It was already dark when we left, and snowing gently. We were riding a school bus provided by a local private carrier. For some reason, our own school district buses were not available so the district contracted out for this trip. (As a rookie, I wasn't usually given, nor did I always understand, the reasons for such things.) The ride was uneventful until we left the highway and began traveling the Albany city streets to the game site. Sitting in a front seat (teachers always ride shotgun), I began to notice that the bus was weaving a bit and failing to stay in lane. Some of the students noticed it too.

I engaged the driver in conversation to determine if he was completely in control of himself and the bus. His responses were coherent but seemed a bit 'fuzzy' to me, as if dulled by fatigue or possibly even by drink, though I smelled no alcohol. We were only a few blocks from our destination; I hoped that directing my chatter toward him would keep him awake or at least more focused. Knowing that I had no authority to make him stop the bus on a city street, and fearing an argument if I insisted, I concluded that the best plan was to co-pilot for him, loudly and firmly and watching him closely, till we got to the school. I made sure that he missed no turns and got to the Academy without incident. After we parked and the kids got off the bus, I swore to myself that none of them would board it again. Good call…but how to make sure it worked out that way?

I'd never had the responsibility for the safety of forty or so teenagers hit me so hard. Obviously, returning with that driver was not an option. After killing the engine, he'd slumped over the wheel and had either gone to sleep or passed out. Fortunately I had some time – the rest of the J.V. game and the entire varsity contest – to work on an alternative.

In those pre-cell phone days, I had to ask to use a school phone to call back home…but call whom? No one would be at school at that time of night, let alone someone who had the authority to make things right. I had no home numbers for anyone who could.

After calling directory assistance for the out-of-town numbers, I dialed the principal at home (an act of courage in itself for a rookie), only to find no one there. The vice-principal, Mr. Morrison, was home and, thankfully, knew the bus company owner personally. He'd make that connection; my job was to make sure that, no matter how long it might take for the owner to get to the game with a fresh driver, no students would re-board that bus.

Other than the ice-ball in my stomach when I first figured out that our driver wasn't up to par, and that I'd have to deal with it, I remember only a few things about that night. I remember missing both games, having spent the entire time either on the phone or in the lobby waiting for the bus company owner, whom I didn't know and wouldn't recognize, to arrive with his relief driver. I remember hoping it all was resolved before it was time to leave for home and I'd have to explain to the spectators that I couldn't let them board the bus. I remember watching from a respectful distance as the owner put the original driver in his car and left, and as the relief driver climbed aboard to warm up the bus for the ride back. I remember reassuring some observant – and concerned – students that going home would be a lot less dramatic.

And I have always remembered to tell young chaperones never to supervise an out-of-town trip without first arming themselves with the name and number of every conceivable emergency contact person who might be of some use to them.

I wish somebody had told me that, way back when.

December Observation

When I began teaching in 1972, we had no formal mentoring program. Different veteran teachers gave me great advice through the years, and they have my lasting gratitude. Perhaps the most practical advice came from the man who'd hired me (and seven years later, my wife-to-be), my first principal, George Corrigan Sr. I really took three pieces of his advice to heart, and they made all the difference in my career.

The first one, about getting as involved in extracurriculars as you are able, has been mentioned. His actual words went like this: "I don't care how good your college prep was. You're going to be a liability for a year or two until you figure out how it's done. Everybody is. So you need to find other ways to make yourself valuable so we have a reason to keep you around if we have to make job cuts."

That explains why I have been involved in so many ways with the life of the school. At first I was just playing defense. Then I discovered that I liked it and that it made the day-to-day classroom routine so much more pleasant.

At some point early on, he also advised, "Rick, this isn't like St. Mary's here (my parochial school home, which he'd also attended). These are great kids, but they won't all show up eager to learn. Some won't even be willing. You've got to *perform* your subject, be a bit of an actor, a storyteller."

Though this sounded very challenging to a first-year teacher who'd been in exactly one stage play in high school, with only seven lines to learn, it made sense. I was already hearing tales of how engaging a teacher Mr. Corrigan himself had been in his classroom days, and he taught *chemistry*. I figured that with all the great stories I'd be teaching, the wonderful dramas and timeless issues I'd share, so ripe for analysis, I'd have plenty of fuel for discussion, debate and performance. As it turned out, I was right – and so was Mr. C. The power of story, both classic and personal, has helped me hold kids' attention for many years.

They aren't likely to applaud when the bell rings ending your performance, but if you can look them in the eye as they get up to leave and see the wheels turning in their heads, that's gratifying enough.

Mr. Corrigan's third bit of advice took on a bit of a warning tone: "Just like the man who pulls his hand out of a bucket of water and leaves no lasting impression…if something were to happen to you, we'd have somebody else behind your desk within the week. Sad but true. It has to be that way. Remember, there is no indispensible man."

Those words sound harsh, but I don't believe they were meant to be. Nor do I remember what I had done (or not done) to prompt him to say them. I suppose I found it a bit ironic that he'd earlier encouraged me to get involved as much as I could in the school, making myself as indispensible as possible to secure my job, only to hear him say later on that "There is no indispensible man." It was all a bit confusing.

Regardless, I suppose I needed to hear those words, and I'm glad I did. They have been my main motivation for my entire career. I took on so many roles and wore so many hats over the years just because I didn't want to be that guy who could be so easily replaced. And I've offered similar advice about getting involved in school life to any young hires whom I thought would listen.

You might say that my whole career has been spent trying to justify the confidence my first principal – the man who hired me – had in me. And you'd be right. We all should have someone whose confidence we strive endlessly to justify. For me, George Corrigan was the guy.

January

"See everything. Correct a little. Ignore much."

- Pope John XXIII

Junior Prom 1980
No wedding ring yet.

Junior Prom 2004
Still going strong!

January Lesson

Wednesday, 1/7/09

Yesterday I ran the scoreboard and game clock for our three levels of boys' basketball (freshman, J.V., varsity) as I've done for years. At halftime of the freshman game, a man made his way toward the scorer's table from the bleachers across the court. As he came closer he smiled and extended his hand. I recognized him immediately:

Jim C., class of '79, parliamentarian of our Student Council (of which I was advisor), and an outstanding three-sport athlete. He was there to watch his son, a member of our opponent's team.

After a minute's reminiscence he said, "You know, I've often said to myself that if I ever saw you again, I had to tell you this. One time when I was in your class you told us that the National Anthem they play before our games probably didn't mean much to us then, but that it would come to mean more, that we'd appreciate it a lot more as we got older. I've realized the truth of that for a long time now, and I think about that whenever they play it before a game. I knew I had to tell you, if I got the chance, that you were right, it really means more and more to me as time goes by. I just wanted you to know."

How about that? I didn't recall saying that but he, and maybe others, remembered it for thirty years and had come to see the Anthem not as something that delayed the game he'd come to play or watch, but as symbolic of something that makes those games possible, and that getting on your feet as it begins playing isn't a duty but a privilege.

What amazes me isn't so much that he remembered it but that, at age twenty-five or so, I had the good sense to say it.

January 1980

Welcoming Committee

In a perfect world, we'd never hold colleagues accountable for things that we ourselves haven't mastered, never expect more from beginners than we were able to handle when we were in their shoes. But the world isn't perfect, and neither am I (far from it), so I got it all wrong. But only that one time, and I got away with it, and then some.

Getting the kind of quiet you need in a classroom in order to administer a major test isn't easy for a new teacher. They never seem to cover that sort of "nuts and bolts" stuff in college ed courses; you pick it up from your host teacher during your pre-service semester, or maybe ask a veteran once you've landed a position of your own. It might be as simple as re-arranging the physical space in the classroom or as complex as finding your "teacher voice" and the timing that goes with it. As a wily veteran in my eighth year, I had all of that down pat. Unfortunately and unfairly, I expected that everyone else on staff would, too. I'd forgotten about the rookie next door.

We were about halfway through a unit test on *Macbeth* when we could no longer pretend to ignore the rising volume coming from Room 39 next door. Period 3 English

10 Honors was getting concerned; concentration was getting more difficult, with predictable results: difficulty concentrating = lowered test grades = parent complaints to the school = me in the office with "some 'splainin' to do." That's often the way it goes with Honors students…and with Honors parents. With the pained eyes of struggling test-takers on me, it was time to act.

Putting my finger to my lips in a request for silence, and leaving my door open to discourage those inclined to cheat, I strode purposefully to the offenders' door – about three strides from my own – yanked it open and declaimed,

"CAN WE HAVE SOME QUIET IN HERE, PLEASE? I HAVE SOPHOMORES NEXT DOOR TAKING A UNIT TEST!"

I hoped the reference to sophomores would help persuade the noisy frosh to co-operate. I also hoped my sophomores would hear it and know I'd gone to bat for them.

After glaring around the room for a sufficiently menacing moment, I strode back to Room 41. The test resumed, the scores were satisfactory, and no parent calls ensued.

I make no mention of the teacher of that noisy freshman group because at that moment she was simply not on my radar. She had replaced a good friend and colleague who'd taken a guidance job elsewhere just before Thanksgiving. We had no free time together to get acquainted, and because I was busy coaching basketball, I hadn't attended any department meetings with her after school. She'd been teaching in the next room for just over a month; I didn't even know her first name.

I was so intent on getting the quiet my students needed for testing, and proving that I was their advocate, that I acted spontaneously and, I know now, thoughtlessly. Obviously I should've called her to the door, made my case for quiet privately, and hoped for the best. In my lame effort to show off my "chops" for the benefit of my students (and hers, whom I'd inherit the next year) I never considered what effect my outburst might have on her classroom control in the future. Talk about expecting too much from a rookie. Talk about getting off on the wrong foot.

Fortunately, though I didn't apologize for this heavy-handed intrusion-cum-introduction, she forgave me. We began dating that summer, and were married the following July.

Whenever "first-encounters-with-spouses" tales are told at parties with friends and colleagues, I cringe a bit; I know our story will end with heads shaking in disapproval and looks of "How could you ever forgive that?"

Twenty-nine years later, I still wonder about that myself.

Oh, and her name is Elisa. Still the prettiest name ever, in my opinion.

January Observation

A question I've sometimes gotten during my tenure as a high school teacher is, "What's it like being married to a person that you also go to work with every day?"

For us, it was never a problem. Sometimes it was an advantage, even a blessing. I believe Elisa would agree. We'd both add, though, that it depends on whom that other person is.

I've known some teachers whose teacher-spouses work in other districts. I've known those whose spouses work in the same district, including ours, but in different buildings and at different levels. I've known some whose spouses work in the same building but in different departments. And I can think of three couples (including Elisa and me) who've worked in the same building and department. To take it one step further, for a time we even taught the same subject and levels in alternate years. Familiarity may breed contempt for some; for us, it has bred respect.

Once we got past our somewhat rocky first encounter (see "Welcoming Committee") in January of 1980, we were cordial, though not yet dating. Our first "date" was when we stepped out together after having been seated at the "singles" table (sort of like the Thanksgiving Day "kids table," only taller) at the retirement party of George Corrigan, the principal who'd hired us both. The date: Friday the 13th of June, 1980. Not the most promising date to begin a relationship, but in retrospect the second luckiest day of my life. The first? 7 – 11 – 81, our wedding day.

It was relatively easy during the 1980-81 school year to keep our deepening relationship "off the radar." Students wondered why two unattached teachers working in such proximity to each other (i.e., next door) weren't getting together. Some even asked openly, trying to play matchmaker. The cat stayed in the bag until our February 1981 engagement. The ring, of course, gave it away.

By that point we were comfortable with people knowing. We had definitely not wanted our relationship to be the subject of speculation, speculation about such things being practically a national pastime in high schools, particularly among female students. This is not to say that such relationships were common in our school at the time, or that it was a latter-day *Peyton Place.* I never had a clue about such things, never was the guy to whom colleagues would run with tidbits of juicy gossip. I usually found out about that sort of stuff, if I found out at all, well after its newsworthiness had passed. That's OK. The gossip loop, whatever the topic, is one that is best to be left out of. Keep your standards higher than that.

One last point: nobody understands your job, its demands and commitments, its pleasures and pains, like another teacher. Especially the one you're married to.

February

"80% of success is just showing up."

- Woody Allen

Le Sabre 2009 Dedication

It is with great pleasure that the staff of Le Sabre 2009 dedicates this book to...

Mr. Pepe

They say he bleeds Schalmont green. Known to many as the voice of Schalmont, Mr. Pepe has been sharing his love of literature, his sense of humor and his passion for teaching with our school community for over three decades. In his 37 years at Schalmont, he has worn many hats, including girls basketball coach, girls softball coach, Student Council advisor, class advisor and DJ extraordinaire. He will forever be remembered by former students for his tremendous passion and by his colleagues as a mentor and friend who is mellow and kindhearted but stubborn when it counts. The staff of Le Sabre 2009 proudly dedicates this book to Mr. Pepe for his lifelong love and passion for teaching.

Dedication.

Sometimes you get it, if you have lived it.

February Lesson

Sunday, 2/8

Spent the afternoon today bowling in support of our Athletic Association's second annual fund-raising tournament. As bowlers go, I'm a complete hacker. My dad averaged over 200 well into his seventies, and my son helped our school team win the NYS Section 2 Class B sectional tournament. I guess the bowling gene skipped a generation. As bad as I am, it felt right to show up, pay the modest entry fee, and show the sports boosters my appreciation. After all, they have always given me a fair hearing, and their financial support, whenever I'd attend one of their meetings to ask for their help in getting some equipment that I "just had to have," and for which I'd forgotten to budget.

It was well worth it. I had fun, got to know some sports parents I hadn't met, saw some old friends, and got thanked repeatedly for coming; it turns out I was the only coach who did, which I did not anticipate.

I think the lesson here is a little bit about showing gratitude for past help freely given, and a lot about seizing the moment. I went partly to lend my support and partly because as retirement nears, I may not have as much chance or as much reason to do it in the future. Though I plan to continue coaching softball after retiring from the classroom, I cannot know for how many more years that will be possible. This was a now-or-(possibly) never situation, so I jumped at it.

One needn't be facing retirement, and dwindling opportunities, to show appreciation to those people and organizations – school-related or not – who have loyally supported us as coaches and teachers. Why wait? You haven't got forever…believe me.

Sunday, 2/15 – It's rare when you find a few lines in a book or a piece of film that encapsulates exactly what you believe, or sums up your philosophy about any subject, much less what you hope your entire career has been about. But I have found one.

This afternoon, Elisa and I watched an episode of *The Twilight Zone* called "The Changing of the Guard," originally broadcast in June 1962, starring Donald Pleasance and written (God bless him) by Rod Serling. I have no memory of this particular episode from "back in the day." Unless the show featured stranded astronauts, time travel or eight-foot aliens kidnapping humans to use as food, I wouldn't watch it, much less remember it. I'm glad I stumbled upon this particular gem today, at this point in my life.

Pleasance is outstanding as Professor Ellis Fowler, who is being forced to retire by the trustees of the exclusive prep school where he's taught for fifty-one years. Something about "youth must be served," according to the headmaster who delivers the bad news. Fowler goes home for the evening and, after a moving oration to his housekeeper in which he describes himself as a failure who's had no impact on his students, brings back a pistol to campus intending to do himself in.

He proceeds to his empty classroom where, in typical *Twilight Zone* fashion, rows of former students, most long dead, appear and assure him that it was he who'd inspired them to face death with courage, or undertake dangerous medical research for the good of others, or sacrifice self to save others in battle, and the like. In the end he sees that though he could point to no personal victories, through his work he could share in all of theirs. His own words, and the literature he chose for them, had inspired them in ways he never suspected. He embraces the impending retirement, uplifted by the knowledge that he has made a difference after all.

Though I have no illusions that I've done even one-tenth the good that Prof. Fowler did, I feel kind of sad that career teachers rarely get to hear from their students about the good that they've done while they're still around to appreciate it. If I were a teacher-trainer, I'd show this episode to all my young aspirants. Hopefully they'd come to understand that the life-lessons that they impart can bear fruit long after each forty-week school year ends. Of course, they might also figure out that it could be many years before they can be certain.

February 2006

The Needs of the Many

Sometimes in life you get credit for things you don't deserve, though Lord knows we all fail to get the credit we do deserve *way* more often. I think when you get undeserved credit or praise it's best to set the record straight.

I had been scheduled without first being consulted, as have many of my colleagues, to sit in on a CSE (Committee for Special Education) meeting, since it is required that any student being evaluated have one of his or her regular classroom teachers in attendance. Scheduled not by the principal (who needn't consult with me or anyone else except perhaps as a courtesy) but by members of the special ed department, during one of my English classes, which I found curious. This most recent time I responded by saying, Sure I'll come, but only if it's during my study hall or my lunch period. The response to my offer was positive and a bit incredulous. You'd give up free time rather than class time for a meeting? Sure I would – but the reason isn't pure altruism.

Having someone cover your study hall is no sacrifice at all; no instructional time is lost no matter who is sent to cover it. Lunch is easy to do without. One less grilled-cheese sandwich would probably do me good.

Turning over your class to a sub in order to put in an appearance at a CSE meeting strikes me as fuzzy thinking. A little-known substitute is not an effective replacement for a veteran teacher. In fact, even a willing veteran from a different content area will likely not communicate your content as well as you would, no matter how detailed your lesson plan. So the class of perhaps twenty-five students is shortchanged to satisfy a mandate to be at meeting focused on *one* student, and comment briefly on his/her progress in your class only? Highly illogical, as Spock would say.

If you believe as I do (and as Spock does) that "the needs of the many outweigh the needs of the few...or the one" (*The Wrath of Khan*), you might agree that giving up your lunch might not be such a bad idea. Or better yet ask the committee, if their meeting time is locked in, to ask a teacher who is "free" at that time to switch places with you.

I'm completely in favor of helping the special-needs student to achieve at a higher level – just not at the expense of a much larger group of peers. Especially when there are alternatives which, though perhaps more complicated to execute, would better serve the needs of the many.

Invite me during my non-teaching time, and I'm there. Spock gave up his life for the needs of the many; I certainly could give up that grilled-cheese sandwich or that breakfast bagel for the good of the one.

I'm not sure what the special ed teachers thought of all this... but I know Spock would approve.

February Observation

I sincerely hope that my friends in special education do not draw the unintended conclusion from the preceding flashback (should any ever see it) that I somehow under-value their assistance in dealing with special-needs students. That should not be inferred; it isn't what I'm implying at all. Certainly I would have been much less successful in the second half of my career, after special-needs kids had begun being mainstreamed, without their advice on how to modify lessons and tests for these kids. I had no clue what to do.

I had never, in college or grad school, been required to take a course on "exceptional" students– on whichever end of the exceptionality spectrum they might be found. Once special-needs students routinely began to be placed in the "least restrictive environment" (i.e., mainstream classes), I was in dire need of help from colleagues who had expertise that I lacked, having trained in a more modern era – that is, more modern than mine (1967-72).

My all-time favorite student success story involves just such a student. Gary was not classified as a special ed student, though in my opinion he would have been had he attended school in a more "enlightened" time – say, the 1990's or 2000's. Since his story took place in the 1970's, when very few students were screened for enrollment in our single self-contained special ed class, Gary was placed in the lowest of our four academic tracks: "Basic" English, designed primarily around survival reading and writing skills. There would be no NYS Regents diploma for him. Gary was a nice, respectful kid, a good athlete and a popular boy who stayed out of trouble and did well enough in his Basic-level classes.

One spring day, one of our guidance counselors approached me in the hall with Gary in tow. When it became clear that they'd been looking for me, we headed for a quiet spot to chat. Jim, the guidance guy, began with a statement.

"Gary plans to go to VO-TECH next year, and we're trying to make that fit into his academic schedule."

"Good. Great. I think that's a great idea for you, Gary," I replied, wondering what it had to do with me.

"Here's why we need to speak to you," Jim continued. "Gary's VO-TECH program is offered in the morning, and the English course that Gary has been taking is also only offered in the morning." Since the Basic students were few in number, only one section was needed.

"I didn't know that," I responded, which was true. At that point, though teachers knew what they'd be teaching in the fall, they didn't yet know at what times those classes would be scheduled. As a guidance counselor with student scheduling to work out (by hand, in those pre-computer days) Jim had the inside scoop.

"So in a nutshell, Gary needs to take English in the afternoon. The best option left for him is to be in your NR (non-Regents) class in the afternoon. It's a step up in difficulty, but we talked it over and Gary assures me he'll work extra hard if it's OK with you to put him in there."

"How do you really feel about this, Gary?" I asked.

"Mr. Pepe, I want to go to VO-TECH so bad, I'll work real hard in your English, I promise."

Though I hadn't taught Gary before, I'd heard him to be an honest kid, a straight shooter whose future definitely would be in the manual trades. He was so earnest, I knew I had to approve the switch. You have no right to derail a student's dream simply because helping him reach it may mean a little bit more care or effort on your part.

It's my favorite student success story because Gary kept his word, worked hard, never got discouraged by the step up in difficulty and, though straight A's were not in the cards, he never was in danger of failing, never was even the lowest scorer in the class. And in those days before consultant teachers' advocacy, he did it all on his own. I'm not sure I was much help, not yet having trained colleagues to advise me *how* to help.

I enjoy telling this story more than I do the stories of more gifted students who've gone on to careers of academic excellence and distinguished service. Today Gary is a successful tradesman. He may never make our Alumni "Wall of Distinction" but he still makes me proud.

March

"Find a job you love, and you'll never work a day in your life."

- Old Proverb

Schalmont High School

Rotterdam New York

This Certifies That

Richard Samuel Pepe

Has satisfactorily completed the requirements for Graduation as prescribed by the Board of Education for the High School and is therefore awarded this

Diploma

Given this twenty-sixth day of June, two thousand and nine.

President Board of Education

Superintendent of Schools

Principal

My honorary diploma–
the first and only (so far).

March Lesson

Monday, 3/2/09

Softball tryouts begin today. Thank God! I don't feel fully useful unless I have an extracurricular activity to plan for and carry out. That's why, a year after I bid farewell to the Class of '76, I took on the job of Student Council advisor and kept it for twenty years.

I thought this pre-season would never get here...I've had two not-so-hot seasons recently to redeem, and the sooner the better. Talk about irony! It felt weird to be recognized by the New York State Section 2 Softball Committee at their 2007 sectional tournament ceremony for my "Outstanding Contribution to Softball" just days after wrapping up a five-win season, our lowest victory total since 1977. As if to confirm the wisdom of their choice, we went out and won seven more in 2008. There were lots of reasons for those numbers, all of them valid; still, I'd rather go out as a coach with a bang than a whimper. If I go out, that is.

There is a precedent here for allowing retirees to continue coaching their teams. Two of my closest colleagues have done it, and I hope to join them. Let's hope the school board permits it, and that they base their decision on my thirty-six year record rather than on these last two seasons.

Friday, 3/27 – My final "Staff Development Day". Lots of folks who know I'm contemplating retiring ask me if I'm glad, or tell me I'm lucky. Actually, I don't feel lucky.

This type of day is a hit-or-miss affair: "hitting" when the in-service work addresses a personal need or interest, "missing" when it doesn't. All in all, I've enjoyed most of them, and found others irrelevant to my situation, my classes or my interests. Consistently enjoyable, though, has been the camaraderie and the exchange of ideas with my colleagues. That never gets old. My worst fear about retirement is the gradual curtailment, if not the outright end, of these work relationships that have made the lame days bearable and the good ones, outstanding. Surely, these people have had as positive an effect on me as the students have. What will I do without them?

Tuesday, 3/31 – The third-ever meeting of the "Alumni Wall of Distinction" selection committee, which decides which alumni are deserving of lasting recognition in the high school's honor court for their contributions to humanitarian causes, their professional excellence, their leadership and innovations in their particular fields, and the like – generally, for their value as role models and inspirers of our current students, and of those to come. I'm a charter member of the committee, having been asked to serve beginning in 2007, the fiftieth anniversary of the school district. I think I was asked because I'd been teaching there for thirty-five of those fifty years. I've continued to serve because I get a kick out of poring over pages and pages of impressive achievements of our graduates, many of whom I've taught, some of whom I remain in contact with. This can be a tedious job, but I love it because it proves over and over that our work is important and does bear fruit. We do not see most of that fruit ripen, but when we do, how sweet it is!

Most memorable for me was the induction of Mike S., a former student and Student Council president of mine who, in his induction speech, thanked the teachers who had impacted him, mentioning what it was that he had taken away from each one named. In my case, he remembered "Mr. Pepe, who taught me that it's possible to be a ballplayer and to love Shakespeare at the same time". Not only had Mike been a standout three-sport athlete in school, he'd spent significant time in pro baseball's minor leagues. He still tells me more frequently than any student I've had of the delight that our time reading *Romeo and Juliet* brought him, which delight continues even today.

I'm glad not everyone realizes how gratifying it can be to be a teacher. The ranks would have been full and I might never have had the chance to experience moments like that.

March 2009

Sparring With the Boss

Having a few years under your belt can be very empowering. So can your imminent retirement.

While chatting with our superintendent about the stipend given to retirees for their unused sick days, I joked that it was too bad that the number of days was capped at three hundred fifty since I, never having taken a sick day, had piled up well over six hundred.

She complimented me on my attendance record and, ever a fan of verbal sparring, came back with this:

"I have to wonder, though, how many students you've infected through the years by not staying home when you didn't feel well."

Obviously intended to be funny rather than insulting, it still took me a few seconds to frame a response – but it was a gem:

"I prefer to think of the over $50,000. I've saved the district by not having to pay substitutes for me all those years."

She's a sharp lady and it's fun sparring with her, but you'd better have your facts straight. I'd had an amount of money already in mind because I'd anticipated some non-teacher who wouldn't be paid for unused time taking a shot at me. I wanted to be able to prove I'd done way more good than harm and that I'd saved the district more than double what the stipend was worth.

I just never thought I'd have to explain that to our superintendent.

March Observation

This quote often attributed to Davy Crockett rings true for me: "Be sure you're right, then go ahead." Great advice for anyone at practically any time, but especially relevant to anyone considering retirement, particularly from a career you've loved.

My decision was not based on personal finances. I did not choose teaching for its great earning potential. Nor did I choose it for the possibility of promotion. No matter how hard you may work at your craft, how skilled you may become, your salary bump in any given year is pretty much the same as any other colleague's. Nor was it the elevated prestige that teaching confers, for though there is a certain amount of respect that comes with long service from within the profession, in the community you may as well work in a warehouse, especially nowadays. Except for your former students who, God bless 'em, usually keep you up on your pedestal.

No, I'd hoped the job would bring me joy and personal satisfaction, and I wasn't disappointed. The satisfactions, at whatever point they were experienced, will never go away. The joys, however, are another matter entirely. They were real and memorable, but became more and more offset by increasing mandates, obligations and other "accountability hoops" levied by politicians, the State Ed Department, and "think tanks" whose tanks are always half empty of the things teachers deem essential, it seems. I hasten to add that this most certainly is not a criticism of my district or building administration; that would be shooting the messenger. And it has absolutely nothing to do with the students, who brought me joy right till the end – and still do.

I had not considered retiring four years earlier, when I first became eligible; I was not ready. I had never considered leaving my classroom for the ephemeral "life of leisure" or for another job – even one in education – because I was happy there. And had I stayed but one more year, I would have received additional years of credit toward my pension as an incentive to leave. No one could have predicted that would be offered, of course, but I don't think I'd have stayed anyway.

How do you know it's time? Those modern-day sages Ben and Jerry said it best on a T-shirt: *If it's not fun, why do it?* That was it exactly; for me it was becoming less fun. The academic freedom I'd so loved was gradually evaporating, its place being taken by directives and regulations that curtailed much of the freedom and creativity that I (and others of long service) had enjoyed from the beginning. And I was in a position to put an end to that, at least for myself, and leave with my good memories intact.

If you don't enjoy your work, it suffers. The kids deserve your best.

My earliest hero Mickey Mantle (who in his prime enjoyed the game of baseball like few others) found his game suffering in his later playing days. It's well known that he *couldn't* enjoy it as he once had because of nagging, serious injuries. So the Mick finally retired in 1968…but his last good year was 1964. Folks would say, "Mickey should have retired years ago."

I didn't want anyone saying that about *me.*

April

"Carve your name on hearts and not on marble."

- Charles H. Spurgeon

AFTER *37* YEARS OF TEACHING HE BEGINS A NEW CHAPTER...

PLEASE JOIN US AS WE HONOR

Richard Pepe

FOR HIS SERVICE AND DEDICATION

Retirement Celebration

FRIDAY THE TWELFTH OF JUNE

TWO THOUSAND AND NINE

SIX O'CLOCK HORS D'OEUVRES AND CASH BAR

SEVEN O'CLOCK BUFFET DINNER

MALLOZZI'S RESTAURANT

1930 CURRY ROAD, SCHENECTADY, NEW YORK 12306

~PLEASE RSVP BY JUNE 1 TO CINDY TYGERT ~(518) 355-6110~

SCHALMONT HIGH SCHOOL, 1 SABRE DRIVE, SCHENECTADY

NAME:________________________ NUMBER OF GUESTS:____

____ YES, I PLAN TO ATTEND. ENCLOSED IS $37 PER PERSON.
(CHECKS MADE PAYABLE TO 'CASH')

____ NO, I AM UNABLE TO ATTEND. ENCLOSED IS $___ FOR THE GIFT.

The best retirement invitation ever!

April Lesson

Saturday, 4/18

Today my softball team returned home from an out-of-town tournament with two more victories. Our record currently is 6 and 1. I hope we keep up this pace; it's our best start in years.

Highlight of the day: stopping at Burger King after the games, pulling out my wallet to buy the team lunch since we'd won both games (a promise I'd made beforehand), and having them politely decline my offer – I think they might have been testing me – instead inviting me to join them at an ice cream stand back home that evening for a "team dessert." I brought Elisa there with me and we were pleased to see that the players were not at all embarrassed to be seen with me.

And I wasn't even buying.

Thursday, 4/23 – I was asked today if I'd like to present a scholarship award at Senior Awards Night on May 28th. Every year our high school faculty and our teachers' union each present a substantial money award to two different seniors who intend to major in education at college.

I've not presented an award at Senior Night for over ten years, since retiring as Student Council advisor after many years of presenting much more modest amounts to Council members who'd gone "above and beyond" in their service to the group. I honestly thought I'd never again be a presenter, except perhaps at softball team banquets. I'm sure I was asked because the word is out that I'll be retiring for real in June, and because "it'll be nice to honor the guy his last time around."

I said yes, of course. To represent either our faculty or our union even in as small a matter as this…for me, that *is* an honor. Passing the torch, I suppose, from one ending his career to one seeking to begin the same career has real symbolic resonance. I hope the rest of the seniors get that symbolism.

At least, I hope they're not napping.

Friday, 4/24 – My final classroom observation by my principal. I think it went well; we haven't had our post-observation conference yet, so I don't know what he thought. Really, what was the point? He's just doing his job, I realize…but even if I stunk, what's there to be done about it with one quarter of my final year remaining? He was great about it – he always is – so I didn't see the sense in suggesting that it was a waste of both our time. Maybe, since I haven't officially submitted my letter of resignation yet, they felt an observation was in order in case I change my mind. Who knows?

I'd better get cracking on that letter before they find another hoop for me to jump through.

Tuesday, 4/28 – Today during my "free" period (cute name, completely inaccurate) I found myself wondering what my last day in this classroom would be like. No doubt it will be like most other days – the same people, schedule and places I've experienced all year. I suppose by then the word will get out to the student body – a few know already – and that will change the routine in a way I can't foresee. I hope that they'll be kind, express polite regret, wish me luck, and head for their next class. More likely, they'll say, "Can we have a party?" for which no one is prepared. For them, simply ditching the lesson plan will be enough; chips and soda are always optional, anyway.

Hopefully, there will be hugs.

April 2001

The More Things Change

Once again I was asked to be a part of the committee that would plan the Class of '76 reunion, the twenty-fifth this time. They reunite every five years like clockwork; I can think of no other class during all my time at Schalmont that can say that. The class members would say that it has a lot to do with the climate of pride and togetherness that I tried to instill from '72 through '76 as their advisor. I do appreciate that, but I know it has more to do with their being a very friendly, social group who've easily put aside the drama and cliquishness of adolescence and simply enjoy each others' company. And a good party.

It's a hoot when the planning committee members, tossing out ideas for dates, places and degrees of formality for the reunion turn to me and ask, "What do you think?"

My brain thinks, You guys are all forty-three years old, go ahead and make the decision! What comes out of my mouth is nothing like that, however.

"Well...I think the idea about the hotel ballroom is good, so the travelers can have a room nearby after a late night", or something of that sort.

Their regular attempts to keep me involved are not really necessary but flattering and I appreciate them. Still, it seems silly for a group of forty-somethings who've run their own businesses and planned similar things for their corporate employers to ask a schoolteacher who neither planned nor attended his own prom, and barely managed to put theirs together twenty-six years earlier, for his advice on their reunions. Such is the loyalty forged between a struggling young class-advisor and "his" kids in the crucible of their high school years.

They appreciated my efforts from the start, but many had to get some years on them before they could say so. I am fortunate; some advisors never hear it. Only five promgoers sought me out to thank me personally back in 1975; I still remember their names. But in the ensuing twenty-six years the group has repaid my stumbling novice's efforts many times over.

You don't have to be a genius, or even especially talented, to earn the loyalty of your students. You just have to try. Consistently.

The kids are watching.

April Observation

I was blessed throughout my career to work for principals who gave me space and didn't try to micro-manage what I was doing in my classroom. Only one, the first, had more years in the classroom than I did when it was time for my annual professional observations; none had any background at all in my subject area. It's safe to say that, though some of their suggestions helped me to become a better classroom manager, none had much to offer by way of making me a more skilled English teacher. That was too far out of their own content areas. Their reviews of my lessons were positive and complimentary but were short on content-related pointers. As one principal put it, "You've been doing this for over thirty years. What can *I* tell *you* about teaching English?"

Attending the NYS English Council conferences so many times taught me a few things, the most important being that you're never too old or experienced to learn some new tricks to use to tweak your lessons for the better. I frequently took home from those gatherings notes and handouts that did just that, even after thirty-plus years on the job. *That's* where you look for content-specific suggestions rather than from building administrators, even ones as reasonable and well-meaning as mine. Unless of course your principal or vice-principal used to teach your subject! Better still, look to senior department members or chair-people for such advice. If you work in a building where senior faculty are involved in the observation process, you're most fortunate.

Though being observed and evaluated can be stressful for young teachers, if done by the right people it's the best way to get better.

May

"Good teaching is one-fourth preparation and three-fourths theater."

- Gail Godwin

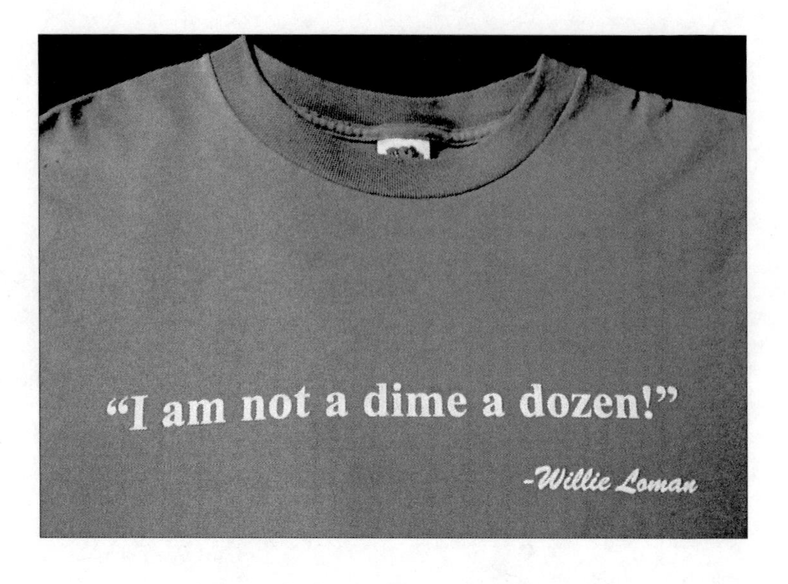

Yes, I know it's 'Willy',
but the vendor had the last word.

May Lesson

Monday, 5/4

Bit of a tough day, today. During my planning period I delivered a copy of my letter of "resignation for the purpose of retirement" to my principal. The official copy would be delivered to the school superintendent later in the day.

I'd written the letter the day before. For a brief little thing, it took a long time to complete, probably because it took so long to force myself to begin writing it. The principal was very gracious, told me how difficult it must have been to come to my decision (an under-statement), shook my hand and wished me well. No mention of my final classroom observation yet.

Upon leaving his office I went to the mailroom to check my box and saw that each one had been stuffed with an invitation to my retirement party. I've seen dozens of such things over the years, of course, and I know the party is being planned; still, the finality of the letter coupled with the timing of the invitation got the day off to a morose start.

It got better later on when Sarah, my young English Department colleague who'd designed the invitation, brought me one of my own as a keepsake. What a beautiful work! Truly the classiest, most dignified invitation I've seen in thirty-seven years. I was, and am, touched, nearly moved to tears...but just *nearly*. To go back into my period 3 classroom, top-heavy with boys, grabbing at the tissue-box just wouldn't do. They'd never let me forget it. Even though we have only six weeks left together (or rather *because* we do), I've got to keep the charade going: business as usual.

Just my luck: today in period six, we watched the final scene of the film *The Miracle Worker* where Patty Duke as Helen Keller, after realizing for the first time that things (and people) have names, breaks away from her mother's embrace to grope her way back to Annie Sullivan who had through hard work and dedication made the breakthrough happen. Helen points tentatively at Annie, asking symbolically, "What name?" Annie, using the manual alphabet she'd taught Helen, spells "Teacher". At that moment, though it was our third day of viewing the film, I realized that it was the last time I'd ever show that wonderful film, so pro-teacher, to a class of students.

Good thing the room was darkened. It was a two-tissue moment.

Sunday, 5/10 – Yesterday our son Dan graduated from college. A terrific day from start to finish. He's an English major but, unlike me, his mom and his sister Christina, he has no firm desire to teach it. His passion is for photography and he's already very good, having shot several friends' weddings and created his own website displaying his handiwork to other potential clients. He's already registered for fall courses leading to a M.F.A. in digital photography, telling us he'd like to teach it someday at the college level in addition to his professional photo jobs.

Dan had asked us early in his sophomore year if we'd mind if he dropped his education courses. The English was fine but he saw no sense in completing the Ed. courses since he thought that was not what he wanted to spend his life doing. He'd figured out that he could with proper credentials teach his passion, possibly even at the college level, while bringing in some additional income on the side. It's a great idea, a great plan.

In a way, I envy him. I've spent thirty-seven years sharing some of the world's great art, in literary form, with my students. It's been well worth it, the transmission of the culture being high on the list of things I believe are important about my job. But, however well I do it, I am still just a conduit for the memories and the art of other (admittedly noteworthy) people. Dan will use his talent to help his clients preserve their own memories and his students, their own art. He will be able to, and will teach others to, stop time and savor it for as long as they desire.

I wish I could do that right about now.

Tuesday, 5/19 – If one more person asks me, "Counting the days?" I'll scream. It's their attempt to congratulate me on my decision to retire, and to compliment me on a job (hopefully) well done...or at least of long duration. Even as I understand and appreciate their friendly overtures, I don't *want* to count the days. For most people, doing that implies an eagerness to be done, to finish up and leave. But I am not most people. Though for several reasons it is the right time for me to go, it'll be the hardest thing I've ever done in my life.

Thursday, 5/21 – Tomorrow is the biggest game of our softball season, one we must win in order to qualify for post-season play. I really hope we do. These girls deserve to go; they have already won more games than in the last two seasons combined. Plus, it may well be my last chance to do so as a coach. It would be good to see some old coaching friends again for what may be the final time. But mainly I want these players to go. We've missed out the last two seasons, so none of them has ever been to the postseason tournament. What a nice way for our seniors to finish out their careers. I can relate.

Friday, 5/22 – They did it! A 5 to 1 victory. On to the tournament. We'll find out next Tuesday when, where and whom we'll be playing. Though we all hope for a reasonable opponent and a good game, it doesn't matter. We got our wish. Now, to keep it alive.

Tuesday, 5/26 – A former student, a girl whom I taught last year as a freshman, knocked on my door today during a class. When I said, "Come in", she poked her head in and said on behalf of the two girls standing behind her as well, "We're gonna miss you next year when you retire!" and she was gone. The cat is now officially out of the bag. I hope I can keep the focus on the curriculum for the remaining thirteen days of instruction.

My focus too, not just theirs.

Friday, 5/29 – A rollercoaster of a day. First, the good news. During my free period, a knock on my door preceded the yearbook staff trooping in, led by the two editors, with a new yearbook. Since in our school the new books are given first to seniors at their Senior Banquet, I assume this is an "advance copy." I had no idea why they were there. The best I could come up with was, "Awww, you're giving me a free yearbook because I'm retiring, right? Thank you very much."

The group just smiles, as the editors shake their heads. "Open it," they urge.

On the very first page after the endpaper, there it is – the yearbook has been dedicated to me this year. Not just a donation…a *dedication*! There, above five pictures of me taken from old yearbooks, are the words of dedication, thanking me for the many roles I have played here and for my "lifelong love and passion for teaching." I'm sure my jaw must've dropped about a foot. I thanked them, more heartfelt this time. I think they were smiling, though I couldn't be sure. Something was in my eye.

Whether this recognition was the idea of the yearbook staff or of their advisor, Tracy, I am not sure. In any case to be so honored, whether by colleagues or students, is huge and I shall remember it, and the moment, always.

Later, we played in the softball sectional game that we'd tried so hard to qualify for …and lost. Same score as our victory that got us there, 5 to 1, only we were on the wrong end of it. Our opponent was a larger school from a tougher league. No shame in losing to a team like that. We had a few hits, got an outfield assist, picked off a runner at third base and generally acquitted ourselves well. We simply were outmuscled by stronger hitters and dominated by a college-bound pitcher. There were a few tears afterward, but not many. We'd won fourteen games this season, turning a couple of bad years around, and could make the long bus ride home with our heads up. My pride in my players trumped my sadness in knowing that I might've coached my last high school game. We'll see what the future brings, and whether I'll have the time to come back next year and coach in retirement, as others have done here.

That's not bad – 945 games coached in two sports totaling 51 seasons, and still not tired of it. That's the power and charm of young athletes, some of whom want college careers, most of whom just want fun and good memories of it. I'll drink to that.

A sports drink, of course.

May 2002

"Attention Must Be Paid"

All veteran teachers worth their paychecks realize that they are responsible not only for the learning of their students, but also for that of the rookie teachers who join the team from time to time. I would ask, why not add new administrators to the list of those needing our guidance? Teachers know that college coursework alone is never enough preparation for handling real, live students; you figure it out best by actually doing it. The same is true for school administrators, at least when it comes to relations with staff. Who better than teachers to teach new administrators how best to handle real, live teachers? My own foray into "Staff Relations 101 for School Administrators" may not be for everyone, but it worked for me.

Late-season department meetings can be grueling affairs, dealing as they do with book ordering, testing schedules, grading of state exams, next year's course assignments and the like. When a visitor is expected, or pops in, it changes the dynamic somewhat and adds some novelty to the dull sameness. When Scott, our new assistant principal, dropped in on our meeting to discuss next year's projected enrollment and the number of English course sections which would be offered, the talk turned to staffing needs and potential new hires in our building. Scott mentioned that there again was a shortage of available math and science applicants, but not so in English. "English teachers," he added, "are a dime a dozen."

That put a bit of a damper on the proceedings; the raised eyebrows gave away our reactions to his remark, though no one addressed it until the meeting ended and Scott had left the room. It became clear that no one had liked that remark, all had felt slighted, and some had struggled not to voice their displeasure to him. Having known Scott for a few months by then, we felt sure he'd not meant to offend.

As a thirty-year veteran I had heard teacher-slights coming from administrators before, and they'd bothered me less and less as I matured in the job and gained more confidence. They were harder to hear earlier in my career; implicit messages of derision from an administrator can be especially wounding to a young teacher. I wondered now how my several young colleagues were handling this offhanded blow to their developing professional self-esteem.

As the senior member of the group, I felt duty-bound to spin the situation to our advantage somehow, to send the message that our curriculum is as vital as any other (perhaps more so), that the large number of English Ed majors seeking teaching positions does *not* imply that our training, or what we do, is easy, and that we as a group ought not to be taken lightly, at least not in *this* school. But how to do so?

Over-reacting with a grievance or some other confrontational approach would not do. No, the response must flow naturally from the offending wisecrack and, if possible, convey our message with humor. Replaying Scott's remark in my head gave me the solution, one that would let me go to bat for my colleagues while making our point subtly but clearly. And they would love it. It would take a little bit of time and money to pull off, but it would be worth it.

Several days later when classes were ended, state exams administered and grading of finals underway, our department met to divide up the various sections of the NYS English Regents Exam for team grading, as required. That done, I asked for a minute of their time. Recalling the previous meeting and our collective desire to respond to Scott's remark, I asked them to join me in sending him a gentle, hopefully lasting reminder of how not to treat teachers. Reaching into a small cardboard box I'd brought along, I pulled out one of seven custom-made green T-shirts I hoped they'd join me in wearing as we graded the exam together. Across the chest in white letters was this:

"I am not a dime a dozen!"
Willy Loman

Fans of classic American theatre will recognize this line from Arthur Miller's *Death of a Salesman* as Willy's impassioned plea to his boss to be treated as someone who does his job as best he can, someone whose service deserves to be appreciated, someone who *matters*. And our literate plea to be afforded the same dignity that Willy sought, couched in Scott's own phrase, in our school colors? Perfect!

Thankfully, my colleagues thought so, too. Believing Gandhi had the right idea, we would not be entering school together in a green-and-white show of solidarity, nor wearing the shirts among curious and questioning students (they were gone for the summer), nor haranguing the rest of the faculty in the teachers' lunchroom. We would simply wear the shirt on the agreed-upon grading day, remaining in our workrooms practically the entire time, emerging only for lunch or bathroom breaks. Word would get around. And with luck, Scott would see one or more of us in the hall or the office; we certainly hoped so. We would say nothing about the shirts to other teachers unless asked. (I've no idea what my colleagues might've said to faculty friends. I just said, "Ask Scott.")

The day came and we went about our business in uniform, even the non-tenured newbies (whom I'd told not to participate if they were uncomfortable doing so), which I offer as testament to their courage, if not their good judgment. As point man for our "awareness seminar" I expected I might be hearing from Scott soon.

Two days later, he dropped by my room when I was there alone. We chatted about it all more or less amiably, each of us expressing that the whole business was regrettable, neither of us apologizing. He was not happy but, all in all, was a very good sport about it. He assured me that he'd not meant to offend, which I believed and accepted; I assured him that next year would be a fresh start, and that he'd enjoy his new role more if he gave more consideration to how he was perceived by his staff. Scott stayed on as assistant principal for one more year, the T-shirts made no more appearances, and his relationship with our department was good.

I still find it a bit puzzling that Scott, a former English teacher himself, was not more solicitous of his former calling once he put on his principal's hat. (At any rate, I'm sure he caught the literary reference instantly.) And I certainly never expected to see *Death of a Salesman* play the midwife to the birth of an administrator.

May Observation

Perhaps nothing else enhanced the great career memories I now enjoy as much as coaching interscholastic sports. And of all my many seasons as coach, nothing else compares to 1986.

1986 – what a year for girls' sports at Schalmont! We won the Colonial Council softball championship in late May, then followed it up with the New York State Section 2 championship the following week. The team had built on momentum begun in February, when the girls' varsity basketball team had won the Council trophy and then a week later, the Section 2 title.

As coach during both seasons it's tempting to brag about my role in the 37 – 5 overall record for the two sports, or the league and Section crowns in both sports in the same year, which I'm told no other area coach has ever done. Let it go at that. To say more would not only be unseemly – it would be fishing for more credit than is due.

Naturally, in the course of forty-two total games a coach is bound to have made some smart strategic or personnel moves. Probably a few bone-headed ones, too. If there is a lesson to take from our successes of 1986, it's this: you won't win much without good players, no matter how clever you, yourself may be – but you'll win a whole lot more if they actually *like* each other.

The girls on those teams were closer than any teammates I've coached before or since. Movies together, sleepovers, trips out for ice cream or pizza, all sorts of team bonding activities that arose spontaneously beginning with the junior class, whose numbers dominated both squads, and spread to the others on the team. This was not part of any grand scheme of mine; they knew and liked each other as grade-schoolers, before we'd ever met.

Getting players to put team before self is much easier when that team is loaded with kids who've eaten at each others' tables, shared vacations and swapped secrets. Players who've shared so much off the court or field will more easily share the ball, the precious minutes of playing time, the blame when it's appropriate and the glory when it's earned.

In 1986 we earned a *lot* of glory. In my opinion, no athletes enjoy these moments more than female athletes.

In thirty-seven years coaching interscholastic sports, I've run into several teachers and coaches – home and away and all males, it should come as no surprise – who would never consider coaching a women's team. There are those who have, of course, and done it well; but there were easily even more who ruled it out. Personally, I didn't get into girls' sports in 1974 to make a pro-feminist statement (I was mostly apolitical) or for the money (the pay was terrible). It filled a need, impressed my principal and, win or lose, brought me satisfaction and even joy.

Today there are plenty of men coaching girls' teams at the school and rec levels. Those who do will agree that nothing beats the gratitude and appreciation shown coaches, male or female, by female athletes. I came for the job security and stayed – for fifty-two seasons – for the joy and appreciation.

If you have any sport-specific knowledge or experience I say run, do not walk, to your athletic director when a girls' coaching position opens up, and apply for it.

Win or lose, you won't be disappointed.

*****

One other point about interscholastic sports, on the issue of whether student-athletes should specialize in a single sport or play multiple sports if possible. I must come down on the side of playing multiple sports, if that's what the athlete wants to do. Of course, if the athlete wants to specialize in a single sport, I would encourage that as well – provided it is his/her decision and not dad's, mom's or the coach's.

I have watched students do both for many years and believe that there is a greater experiential value in interacting with the broader range of athletes and coaches afforded by playing two or even three different sports in the course of a high school career. The more personal relationships forged, the more the athlete learns about dealing with a variety of people, systems and competitive philosophies. It can be very enlightening for a star soccer player, for instance, to deal with coming off the bench during basketball season. It gives the "haves" in this situation some perspective on how to cope with what the "have-nots" have already learned to handle. Since we can't "star" at everything in life, this seems a good lesson for kids to take into their futures.

I'm one hundred percent certain that athletes who win championships in more than one sport during a high school career are glad they didn't specialize in just one sport. My personal experience as a coach confirms this to my satisfaction.

And the parents who force a child to specialize against the child's will in hopes of possibly earning a college sports scholarship should have their parenting licenses revoked. It should be the athlete's choice, free from adult pressure. Period.

June

"To love what you do, and feel that it matters…how could anything be more fun?

- Katharine Graham

ROTTERDAM

'Voice of Schalmont' retiring after 37 years

Beloved English teacher never took a sick day

BY JUSTIN MASON
Gazette Reporter

For Rick Pepe, working nearly four decades at a job without taking a single sick day isn't that big of a deal.

The Schalmont High School English teacher credits his impressive string of illness-free days at the district to the good genes and good work habits he inherited from his parents. Besides, it's a bit difficult for him to call in sick to work when he doesn't consider his job work in the first place.

Pepe

"Ever since kindergarten, I've never gotten up to go to work," he said. "I've always gotten up to go to school."

Pepe's streak will end at the district this month, but not because he plans on skipping a day at work. After 37 years with the district, the beloved educator who some call the "voice of Schalmont'" will retire at the end of June.

"I'm still finding every day as interesting and rewarding as it was in the beginning," he said.

The district honored Pepe this week by conferring Schalmont's first-ever honorary degree to him. In doing so, they commended him
first-ever honorary degree to him. In doing so, they commended him
for his wide breadth of service to Schalmont, including 20 years as a Student Council adviser and the adviser to the class of 1976.

In sports, Pepe coached the varsity girls' basketball team for 15 years and the varsity girls' softball team for 36 years. His coaching accolades include a girls' basketball sectional championship, two Colonial Council softball championships and six Colonial Council girls' basketball championships.

The seemingly ubiquitous Pepe also served as the de facto Schalmont DJ during dozens school dances and the announcer for the district's varsity football games. He's typically the master-of-ceremonies for school pep rallies and operates the clock at high school basketball games.

"You name it, he's been here and he's done it all," said High School Principal Terence Nash, who has worked with Pepe since 1999.

Pepe grew up in Amsterdam, where his family ran Pepe's Restaurant, a fixture on West Main Street for 77 years. He attended Siena College before earning his master's degree from the University at Albany in 1972; several months later, he took a job teaching English at Schalmont.

"And I've been here ever since," Pepe said.

Colleagues characterize him as an eternal optimist who treats his
Colleagues characterize him as an eternal optimist who treats his
students with respect and dignity. Nash said Pepe serves as a role model for both the young pupils and his fellow teachers.

"If I had a building full of Rick Pepes, my day would be a walk in the park," he said.

Superintendent Valerie Kelsey also commended Pepe for his outstanding service to the district. She said Pepe is well-regarded by both students and parents, some of whom he taught during his earlier years at the district.

"He is totally committed to the school," she said. "He made his career here."

In retiring from the district, Pepe won't leave education altogether. He plans to teach part-time with the Careers in Education program at the Hamilton-Fulton-Montgomery BOCES. He was recruited to the position by Principal Jay DeTraglia, who worked with him as a student teacher.

Pepe said he'll miss being at Schalmont and still plans to coach softball. But he said he can leave the district with a smile, knowing he's leaving behind a more-than-capable staff to continue his legacy.

"I know the place is in good hands," he said.

Reach Gazette reporter Justin Mason at 395-3113 or jmason@dailygazette.net.
jmason@dailygazette.net.

"Beloved"??

That's really up to the kids...

June Lesson

Monday, 6/1

A surprise e-mail came to me today from our superintendent's secretary inviting me to the Board of Ed. meeting a week from tonight. It seems the Board will be accepting my retirement-resignation at that time, and the superintendent thought it would be nice if I were to attend and be recognized for my service. Of course Elisa and I will be there; it's an honor to be so recognized. Perhaps they do this for all retirees, I don't know. I've never been to a Board meeting with retirees on the agenda. Either way, I'm there. It might even be fun, a bit of a trip down "memory lane." Six of the seven Board members have had children pass through the high school. Of those fifteen kids, I've taught eleven of them, and never was heard a discouraging (or disparaging) word, so the memories all ought to be good ones.

Wednesday, 6/3 – My final general faculty meeting. The usual stuff: construction updates, final exam schedule-tweaking, union business. No mention of my retirement, or that of my long-time colleague, Anne. That's OK. Too-frequent mention of it would just bore people, I think, and they all know by now anyway. And I'm not sure I want to be reminded, myself.

Thursday, 6/4 – Tonight I attended a farewell concert in honor of a colleague from our middle school, a band teacher who is also retiring. Mark conducted a band comprised of one hundred forty former students, town band members and even some current faculty members including Elisa. The sound was titanic, the players inspired, and the anecdotes and tributes flowed freely, punctuated with smiles and tears. A fitting end to an old friend's inspirational career.

It helped that the concert's end was so upbeat, because the beginning had left me in a bit of a funk. The first act featured our eighth-grade chorus, followed by the eighth-grade band. As they filed onstage and took their places, I realized that I'll never get to know them as students in the high school, and it made me sad. I suppose it has to end sometime. My retired former colleagues all tell me that in three short years I won't know any of the students anymore. I'm sure they mean to cheer me up; I just don't think it's working.

Monday, 6/8 – I'm slowly learning that sometimes it's more fun to be in the dark about what's going on than to know everything.

Last week I was informed in an e-mail from our district office that I was invited to the June school board meeting; they wanted to present me with a certificate recognizing my "thirty-seven years of service without having taken a sick day." I showed up there with Elisa and, after a few kind words about my stamina and dedication, I was presented with a very nice certificate to note the occasion. Thinking I was through, I began walking back to my seat.

Before I was halfway there, the superintendent called me back for the "part of the presentation that will come as a surprise." As I returned and stood before them, the Board president began reading a litany of my years spent as advisor, coach and chaperone, my service as scorekeeper, announcer and D.J., and the various championship teams I had coached through the years. I could only wonder where he was going with all of this. Then I noticed my principal making his way to the front of the room, holding what looked a lot like our diploma cover. As he neared me with his hand outstretched, I heard the board president conclude with something about "the first honorary graduate of Schalmont in school history."

That finally did me in. They had managed to surprise me completely with an honor that was the first of its kind. In my few completely unrehearsed words of thanks, I said that I'd rather have that diploma than the keys to a new car (not that I'd turn one down!).

Only when it was all over did I realize why Elisa had *really* invited my parents there from out of town. It turns out that the only one in the dark was me.

Tuesday, 6/9 – Tonight was our annual end-of-season softball awards banquet. Good food, great company and an excellent time for all. I hope I can return to coach again next year but if I can't, this was a great sendoff. I told the team, "If this is to be my last season, I'm glad to have spent it with you," and I meant it.

Thursday, 6/11 – My last actual lesson with my ninth-graders before exam week was to read and discuss Isaac Asimov's 1967 short story "The Fun They Had." It's a cute little tale blending a bit of sci-fi with a completely obvious bit of propaganda to the effect that today's kids are fortunate to have the human interactions at school that their descendants in 2155 AD will not have, being instructed at home by mechanical teachers calibrated to each individual child's needs and pace. Even as I was eliciting their feelings about their own learning styles and experiences and how it all might, though less efficient, be preferable to a soul-less robotic instructor, I began to muse about the social component's impact on *teachers*, and specifically what it had meant to me.

As the kids responded to each other's observations, I concluded that for me the social aspect of a teaching career had been a very big deal. I realized that I'd never again, in all probability, chaperone a prom, operate a scoreboard, D.J. a dance, announce a football game, or M.C. a pep rally or other spirit event. I'd be less likely to attend concerts and drama productions, and maybe even have to give up coaching depending on my future obligations.

I remember being told in college that the proper function of schooling is "the education and socialization of students." Whoever wrote that overlooked one other important thing: the education and socialization of their teachers. Sitting in that long-ago classroom, I could never have anticipated how much the school society would mean to me, nor how much I'd learn about teaching *after* I'd left college with my diploma and my professional certification. Nor that some of my best teachers would be my students.

Friday, 6/12 – My last official day of teaching at Schalmont. Exams remain, but instruction is at an end. Many smiles, cards and good wishes came my way. Period 3 brought goodies for a party in my honor. The stream of well-wishers in each class was gratifying and heartwarming.

Many yearbooks were signed, and the mood was mellow, even reflective, or as much as it *can* be with a roomful of fourteen- or fifteen-year-olds on the last day of class. Not all participated, of course; some were too shy, I suppose, and some others probably just didn't want to let sentimentality ruin what was largely a free period. My favorite comment: "What will the school do without you? You're *everywhere*!"

The highlight of the day came during period four study hall. A knock at the door, and in marched about thirty or so members of our concert choir, their director and their guitar accompanist. On cue, they broke into a stirring acoustic version of The Who's "Pinball Wizard," which they had performed at the Rock and Roll Hall of Fame in Cleveland back in May. I hadn't been able to make that trip because of softball, but would have loved to go. Knowing this, and knowing that it was the last day before this Who fan retired, the director, my friend Bob, brought them in to serenade me. A great song, a great performance and a great farewell gesture from the music department (which I'd been urging for years to get more pop tunes into their shows).

I loved it, and the handshakes and hugs that followed. I'll remember for a long time the looks on the study hall kids' faces, and the one wide-eyed freshman girl who said simply when it was over, "You are *loved*." I know that. I have been truly blessed.

Saturday, 6/13 – Last night, I was told by many who were there, was the most memorable retirement party they'd ever been to. And it was mine.

It began, just before dinner was served, with a gift for me and my family presented by my friend and department chair Kevin C., who was our M.C. for the evening. Our very own concert T-shirts – black of course, with the words *Pepe's Final Tour'09* arcing above a green-and-white guitar logo against a green background (the school colors). And on the back, in place of the usual concert tour dates, a long list of my teaching and coaching awards and honors. At the bottom, this: *The Man, the Myth, the Legend* in a fancy font. The shirt was conceived and designed by Eric, an enthusiastic (and creative!) young teacher, coach and advisor, a man Elisa had deemed "the guy who is most like I imagine you were in your early days before we met." She's right. Coming from him, the shirt has a lot more meaning.

Then, Christina and Dan took to the podium where each gave a brief but heartfelt speech laced with plenty of humor about growing up in a home with a dad who "turned every trip to the supermarket into a class reunion" and who "taught me to pay off my disputed parking tickets in pennies." Then they introduced a clip from *Sesame Street*: the doo-wop group *14 Karat Soul* singing "You'll Love School" – a song that I, as teacher and doo-wop fan, had sung to them dozens of times as grade schoolers and even, occasionally, in that supermarket.

After a pleasant meal, I tried to make my way around to all the guest tables to thank everyone who had come to help me celebrate. I'd hoped to linger at each table for awhile before the adult guest speakers began, but couldn't get to all of them. Elisa later told me that there were eighteen tables in all, and about one hundred fifty guests who were able to make it. I should've moved faster, but so many asked what the future holds for me that I couldn't. I remember thinking they seemed happier than I did. And probably were.

Next up were our principal, Terry, and one of his predecessors, Mike. They were funny and complimentary, expressing their gratitude for all of my service over the years.

They seemed especially grateful that I'd always handled my own discipline issues. I know a big part of their job is handling discipline for those who struggle with it. I wouldn't want that job "for all the tea in China," as Grandpa used to say. I admire them for taking it on, but it's not for me.

Then up came Jay, my student-teacher in '93 who is now, after a few years in the classroom, the director of a local BOCES vocational school where he has asked me to work part-time in retirement, teaching seniors who seek to become teachers or school counselors all about the profession, the "nuts and bolts" of being a pro *before* they go off to college and learn all of the theory and philosophy that they will later complain does not help them very much when they finally have to run a classroom of their own. (We have all done it; why pretend otherwise?) The program is called *Careers in Education*, and the prospect of showing the ropes to a roomful of twelfth-graders who are really motivated to hear what I have to say has a certain appeal. It would be an interesting change.

Robyn and Mark spoke next. As freshmen when I started out in 1972, they were members of the Class of 1976, and being its advisor was my first extracurricular duty – but not really a duty at all. They were so very eloquent about how much they'd learned, whether in English class or working on class projects, from a mere twenty-two year old that I was deeply moved. I've known for a long time that, as teachers, our words have a terrible power to hurt and a wonderful power to heal and empower our students, but hearing from them personally in front of family and colleagues just how much they'd benefited from *my* words so long before was astonishing.

Whatever else students may or may not take from our words, I learned this: they will not forget them, for better or for worse. I am very fortunate that despite my very shaky lessons early on, something in the delivery did some good. Robyn and Mark would tell you it was the common touch, the personal example, the willingness to befriend them, or the effort to be fair to all. Personally, I think it was the grace of God. How else to explain a twenty-two-year-old nervous rookie's impact being so clearly remembered by fifty-one-year-old former freshmen?

They were followed by Shari, another former student who is now a principal in one of our elementary schools. She reflected on how, though she'd not been one of my many athletes or officers, I've always remembered her when we meet even years later out in the community, and how that makes her feel. It just proves that your students don't have to be young stars to be memorable, and that many will eventually outshine the "early bloomers" given time and the opportunity.

Next up was Steve, my former student who is now our town supervisor. After some humorous observations about me from the early days, he presented me with a framed proclamation congratulating me on my retirement, bearing the official town seal, as well as letters of congratulations from our state senator and assemblyman (also a former student!).

After that, a rousing game of *Pepe-ardy*, the mock-game show creation of my long-time hall-mate Kevin M., wherein three contestants answered questions (or more accurately, provided questions) using titles of rock songs. This was Kevin's clever homage to my reputation as the go-to guy for music trivia. Naturally, I was a contestant and naturally, I won. The fix was in. Thanks, Kevin!

Elisa then introduced a wonderful short slideshow, with appropriate rock music soundtrack, using pictures taken throughout my teaching and coaching career. It was put together by Dan's best friend Kyle (also a former student) with Dan's help, and it was superb. Elisa supplied the photos, but her introduction was absolutely the best part. She told of the power of storytelling in the classroom, and how she first got a hint about the kind of person I was as she overheard my stories coming through the wall separating our classrooms. Again, be careful what you say in the classroom. There may be a lovely new single teacher eavesdropping from next door, and you may end up marrying her. It worked for me.

The evening wound down with a re-enactment of the honorary diploma-award from Monday night, courtesy of our superintendent and principal; the presentation of a gift from our teachers' union; and the presentation of gifts to me from our English Department and presented by Beth, my oldest (longest?) friend there, and soon to be its senior member. The gifts were thoughtful, generous and extremely moving. Most were related in some way to my favorite book to teach, *To Kill a Mockingbird,* and some proclaimed me the "Atticus" of the department. I can't imagine a greater honor than to be mentioned in the same breath as Atticus Finch.

I have noticed that at past retirement parties I've attended, most if not all gifts for the retiree have celebrated the life to come, much like a bridal shower. Almost all of my gifts celebrated the life I will be leaving, more like a bachelor party. I wouldn't have had it any other way.

My closing speech was loaded with thank-yous, pop-culture references (much like my classes), and a few laughs. Those who cared to mention it later on said they liked it, using adjectives such as amusing, funny, heartfelt and the like. For me, only one word will do: inadequate. No ten-minute speech can do justice to the friends and memories cherished over thirty-seven years, not when some of those memories and friends are there in the room with you, and even part of the program. The party was far beyond what I'd expected, and way more than I deserve. And I shall never forget it.

Monday, 6/15 – I went to sleep Friday night believing that the retirement hoopla had finally run its course. Wrong again. *The Daily Gazette,* our local paper, ran an article on me this morning titled "Voice of Schalmont Retiring After 37 Years." True enough, I thought. For several years now Terry, our principal, has been calling me that, it's cute, no harm done. Then, the subtitle: "Beloved English Teacher Never Took a Sick Day." Factually, that's accurate; I guess it is rare to go that long without calling in sick. But "beloved?" To some students, probably. To others, not so much…or maybe, not at all.

Nobody can work in a school for thirty-seven years and not fail to impress, or even alienate, some kids along the way. Kids fail your course. You cut some from teams. You discipline some too harshly, as they see it. You embarrass them without meaning to. You impulsively make promises that you later can't keep.

I don't fault the reporter. He was either covering the board meeting at which I was recognized (his usual beat) or someone in our District Office called him with an angle on a story. It was well-written and factually accurate, and I told him so in an e-mail thanking him for doing it. But "Beloved?"

Maybe it's a good thing I'm retiring. I couldn't take that kind of pressure if I stayed.

Wednesday, 6/17 – Nothing like a pile of NYS Regents exams in English to shrink one's head back to normal size and to anchor one's feet firmly back in reality. One hundred sixty exams? No problem. Four essays apiece? Piece of cake. Each one double-read?

Thank God for team grading! We'll knock these off in what, three or four days? Might as well smile. It's the last time.

I will not miss this particular duty, not even one little bit.

Sunday, 6/21 – Last night we attended the last of five retirement parties held throughout the district. This one honored Frank, a middle school technology teacher (and former softball teammate of mine). In addition to Frank and myself, there were parties for Anne, a high school special ed. teacher; Peter, an elementary school teacher; and Mark, our middle school band director. That's a combined total of one hundred seventy-two years of teaching experience and extracurricular service. There's only one thing you can say to that: Thank you.

On behalf of all five of us: You're welcome!

Tuesday, 6/23 – Three similar episodes, all of them touching in their own way.

The first: While visiting my next-door classroom neighbor Mary, she said, "This may sound strange…but can I have a poster from your room before you go?"

"Sure. Any one in particular?" I asked.

"I don't know…I just wanted one as a memento."

"Well, let's see which one you might like."

We settled on the poster of the main players in *The Wizard of Oz* movie. It was a perfect choice, I thought. After nineteen years as classroom neighbors, and a decade as friends before that, I would miss Mary most of all, just as Dorothy would miss the scarecrow, whom she'd known longest, most of all. (A bit of gender reversal there, but a good metaphor even so.)

The second: Later on, Anthony, a former student and currently our CISCO teacher and resident computer guru, walked in as I was at my desk. I expected he was there to remind me to go back into our computer gradebook program to change some incompletes to number grades. Wondering why he couldn't just phone me from his office with that message, I saw him begin to look around my room as if searching for something.

"You've taken most of your posters down."

"Yep, just about," I said.

"I was hoping I might snag a Beatles poster as a souvenir, if you didn't mind. You always had a Beatles poster on your wall, even when I was in your class. But I see you've cleaned the place out."

"Not completely," I responded. "In fact, if you look on the other side of that file cabinet, you might find something that does the trick."

I watched as Anthony went around the cabinet and saw his eyes widen as he saw the *A Hard Day's Night* movie poster with all four Beatle heads, large as life, taped to the side of the cabinet.

"Really? I can have this? You don't want it?"

"No, I won't have anywhere to put it. You take it. One big fan to another." Anthony slowly cut away the backing tape, careful not to slice through the poster.

"Thanks, Rick. When I look at this, it'll remind me of you."

Since this fine student had grown into a fine man and a valued colleague, that was music to my ears. Beatle music, the best kind.

The third: Still later, while rooting through my storage cabinets, I found an old Boston Celtics poster that used to occupy a place of honor in my classroom. Though somewhat the worse for wear, it had been a beauty: kelly green border, leprechaun logo in the center surrounded by the greats of that period: Bird, Parish, McHale, Johnson, Ainge, Walton, Wedman. I decided to show it to Kevin C., our boys' varsity hoop coach and lifetime L.A. Lakers fan. We'd had plenty of friendly banter over the years as to which franchise was more legendary, so the stage was set for a little one-upmanship on my part. Kevin was recording exam grades as I swaggered into his room.

"Huh? Huh? Lookit this. Now *this* was a team!" I insisted, hoping he'd take the bait. Instead, he took a long, thoughtful look at it, checking out the player photos one by one. He responded with a nod and a question.

"Can I have that, if you're not keeping it?"

"What? You *want* it? What happened to the big Laker fan?"

"Hey, I recognize good players when I see them."

Yes, I thought to myself as I put it on an empty desk and headed for the door, and colleagues with whom you've enjoyed a friendly rivalry and many great chats about hoop.

Me too, buddy, me too.

Wednesday, 6/24 – This summer, my building will undergo extensive renovations. In my area, all windows, ceilings and floor tiles will be replaced. Workmen from various contractor operations have begun to appear everywhere, especially now that exams are finished.

I was packing some boxes with textbooks which must be moved for renovations when came a knock at my door. John, our security guard, poked his head in.

"Someone here to see you. Says he's from the Class of '76."

He stepped back out and in came George V., who was doing sheet metal work for one of the contractors and who was, indeed (and still is) a member of the Class of '76, *my* Class of '76, with whom I've had probably the best and definitely the longest-lasting advisor relationship in anyone's memory (at least around here).

We shook hands, reminisced a bit and brought each other up to speed on our families.

He brought up my retirement and I filled him in on the details, the reasons and as best I could, my plans. It was thoroughly enjoyable and, since we both had work to do, all too brief. We shook hands again, wished each other well and parted with a promise to see each other at the next reunion.

Later when I'd been home for awhile and the "retirement thoughts" kicked in, as they have tended to do for weeks now, it dawned on me that George had been in my English class on day one, period one, the first class I'd ever walked into as a "real teacher" in September of 1972, thirty-seven years before. And there he was today, in my room again, book-ending my entire career on one of my last days at Schalmont. You may chalk that up to mere coincidence if you like; I prefer to think that there is a higher power at work. Though a bit eerie, it was both fitting and perfect.

You couldn't make this stuff up. At least, *I* couldn't.

Thursday, 6/25 – My last day. I will be at graduation tomorrow to chaperone as always, but this was the day I closed up shop, brought my personal stuff out to the car, signed out and said my good-byes. After thirty-seven years, it's over. (That was not easy to write.)

Most of the logistical details were easy. The good-byes were something else entirely. With my acquaintances, it was difficult; with my closest colleagues, murder.

I left at 12:30. The morning was an emotional stew, consisting of packing up, grade reporting, handshakes, hugs, lots of advice shared with the young, a few stories shared with the veterans, and promises to re-connect after the summer with dinners, at ballgames, and at outings for staff and their families.

At this point in their narratives, some memoir-writers will tell you ruefully that though they plan at first to follow through on their promises to get together with former colleagues, they expect that in time such visits will inevitably grow fewer and fewer until they finally stop altogether, to be replaced with chance encounters at the market or the mall. After all, as John Lennon said, "Life is what happens while you're busy making other plans." What they say may be true in their cases, but not in this one.

As long as there are gatherings to attend, I'll be there with bells on. Wearing green and white, of course!

Friday, 6/26 – Graduation Night: my last official "duty" at Schalmont, though I've never felt it was a duty. Since 1985 we've held graduation at Proctor's Theatre, a classic, ornate venue dating back to the Vaudeville era. My service has been to stand at the foot of the steps leading to the stage and hand each graduate a card bearing his/her name so that the class advisor can announce student names accurately as each walks to center stage to receive a diploma. This way, even if they line up incorrectly, their correct names will be read. As long as there's someone at the foot of the steps to match names to faces, it's foolproof. I'm the guy.

This evening, as always, faculty members not part of the stage party who chose to attend took their seats in the large, floor-level box across the aisle from the graduates on the side where they approach the stage, right behind my post at the foot of the steps. It's an ideal place for them to acknowledge the grads as they file out of their rows and make their way to the stage.

This night in her remarks our superintendent made special note by name of the five retirees who together rendered "over one hundred fifty years of service to Schalmont." When she finished that line, the entire audience began a nice round of polite applause.

As I looked around the theatre, smiling, I noticed movement to my left in the teachers' box. All the teachers who'd come to graduation had risen to their feet as they applauded, and were looking at me as they did so. What a feeling! Cynics might say it was merely a show of teacher solidarity as contract negotiations grow nearer; I know better. It was, of course, their tribute to all five of us. You will excuse me if, as the only one of us in attendance, I feel it was more personal than that.

I smiled at them, gave the thumbs-up sign, and turned back to face the stage, several emotions doing battle for control of my face. Oh brother, I thought, if I can't keep it together now, what'll happen when the choir sings the alma mater at the end? Could be a tough few moments for me.

I kept it together. Too many hands yet to shake, the well-wishing mutual this time.

Saturday, 6/27 – It's been apparent to me for years, and especially lately as I approach my sixtieth birthday, that there are things in life that I would've liked to do but never will. I'll never experience the weightlessness of space, nor play ball for the Yankees or Celtics, nor crank out a searing guitar solo before a stadium full of cheering fans. These were the aspirations (or day-dreams) of my much younger self. Instead, I've spent my life at school, trying to have some small impact on the students who've passed through my room, and my life. Looking back, I wouldn't trade that reality for all those other dreams combined.

When my parents took us camping as kids, as our stay came to a close and we were packing up they'd say, "Always leave the site better than you found it."

Others must be the ones to judge whether, as my career at Schalmont ends, I have done that. I know I gave it my best. I hope it was enough.

When I was 14, I knew I wanted to teach, and I hoped I'd find a place where I'd be happy doing it. To say that's what happened is an understatement.

You may say that no place to work is perfect. I'll meet you halfway on that: Schalmont High may not be perfect, but it's been perfect for me.

June 1976

The End of the Beginning

Getting called down to the principal's office is an experience every schoolkid dreads. It's no picnic for teachers either, especially when you're young and have no idea why you've been summoned.

Granted, I'd already had tenure for a year and had a good relationship with Mr. Corrigan, the principal who'd hired me and whom I'd always found to be supportive and fair. Still, he was the *principal.*

"Have a seat, Rick," he said, inviting me into his office. I had no clue as to what he would say next.

"A few of your senior class officers were in here a little while ago," he said. "They asked me if you could hand the class their diplomas at graduation."

This was news to me. Naturally I was flattered and touched to hear it. Their last official encounter with a staff member, and they wanted it to be me.

"I'd be happy to do that," I smiled. What could be easier? Hand each one a diploma, shake hands, and wish each one well. A perfect ending.

"Yeah, well, I told them no, we couldn't do that. The Board of Education president traditionally hands out the diplomas, and I think we'll be keeping it that way. But I told them you could give the keynote speech, and they were satisfied with that. How about it?"

"Mixed emotions" doesn't quite describe my feelings at that moment. Of course, some parting words of advice, of praise, of thanks, of Godspeed would be easy to prepare. It was the *delivery* that concerned me.

I flashed back to the three previous graduations I'd attended since getting the job. Since our tiny gym or modest auditorium wouldn't hold a graduation crowd and, not wanting to turn away family and friends, Schalmont graduations had for some time been held outside on the football field. They may not all have found seating, but as many could attend as desired. With classes of slightly upwards of two hundred students, a crowd approaching one thousand attendees might be expected, possibly more. And I had to speak to them, try to say something memorable, and not mess up. At age twenty-five, the whole idea was daunting. But I said yes sir, of course, love to.

Somehow it all came together. I have no recollection at all of what I said; when I got back to my apartment I tore up my notes and threw the pieces away. There would be no second thoughts about what I'd said, or forgotten to say, or might've phrased more eloquently. No one who was there has ever told me whether they liked it or not, or if they'd expected something different. Maybe that's for the best.

What I do remember is standing up with the class as they were presented to the superintendent for conferring of diplomas, and remaining on my feet throughout that part till every graduate had returned to the senior seats – my small tribute to a class that had entered the school when I had, taught me much of what it means to be a teacher inside the classroom and beyond, and was now leaving me behind.

One other thing I remember: after going home and destroying my notes, I sat silently and alone, thinking about how quickly the first four years had flown, and about how far I had yet to go. These first four, though a period of learning and adjustment, had also been fun thanks to these seniors. Now the real work would begin; I had a career to build, this time on my own.

June Observation

June – any June spent teaching, not just one in which we might consider retirement – seems to bring with it more reflection on the life of the school and your place in it than any other month. For me, the reflections came faster and more furiously in my final year than in any previous one, even though modifications to next year's lessons were absent from them for the first time. There are a few topics late in my final-year journal that were reported but not reflected upon – until now.

Yearbooks

Though I did not buy a yearbook for each of my own high school years (or my college years, for that matter), I bought one for each year of my career at Schalmont, thirty-seven in all. I highly recommend doing this to all young high school teachers; you'll be glad when the time comes to reminisce, to determine when someone graduated and, importantly, to refresh the memory before heading to a class reunion to which you've been invited!

Occasionally I've considered adapting "yearbook writing" into a possible quick-writing assignment on the value of conciseness. Feel free to use the idea; I never did get around to it. It seemed to me it would drain all the fun out of writing in yearbooks to turn it into some sort of lesson, just as analyzing a book or a film in an essay ("200-250 words, typed, double-spaced, 12-point font") kills all the enjoyment to be had in reading or watching it. Just ask the students.

Room Decorations

How boring it must be for students to walk into an undecorated (or under-decorated) room every day. At least they're only there for about forty-five minutes or so. How much worse to have to teach there!

My room-decoration style could be politely described as "schizophrenic." The posters changed from time to time, but the set-up rarely did: in the front, poetry, author pictures, Globe and Greek theatre representations, a *Macbeth* timeline, parts of speech and figurative language (both with examples). Relevant English-y things for my students to look at which would, I hoped, reinforce my lessons.

In the rear, entertainment posters galore: rock bands, star athletes, sports teams I support, classic films, comedy stars. On the side wall, a blend (or clash) of the two cultures, high (literary) and low ("popular"). The fourth wall was the window wall.

Students would come in and say, "Why is all the fun stuff in the back?"

"So I can see it, " I'd say. "I have six periods a day in this room and I want it to be a place where I can enjoy spending so much time. Don't you decorate your room at home so you'll enjoy being there? That's what I'm doing, too."

"Oh."

In my final days at Schalmont, it was a surprise to me when, students having left for the summer, three different and special colleagues were happy to take a poster apiece that had hung in my room – one a film, one a rock band, and one a sports team. And I was happy to share.

And when our town supervisor mentioned in his speech at my retirement party that his mom finally approved of his listening to KISS after he told her *I* listened to them, and then played his KISS ringtone through the microphone, I had no choice but to send him a KISS poster that had hung in my room. It now hangs, I'm told, in his office.

Some might say that it would be more fitting if he had a framed Shakespeare sonnet or an epigram about "courage" hanging there, or that my example caused him to misplace his focus, but *I* wouldn't. He was the *town supervisor,* for crying out loud.

All KISS fans should turn out so well.

Student Teachers

I have volunteered to take on ten student teachers during my career and am happy to say that nine of them were terrific. I did not do so because I felt I had anything special to offer them, but because almost all of them were from my alma mater, Siena College, and I wanted to help the college place them somewhere. To the best of my knowledge, most of them are still fighting the good fight, jousting with the dragons of ignorance.

I believe that once you are a "seasoned pro" you have an obligation to give back to the profession. There are lots of ways to do this, hosting a student teacher being the most obvious. Helping a rookie reflect on his practice helps you, the veteran, to do the same. If that rookie is particularly sharp, you will deal with questions that will cause you to reexamine the rationale behind something you have been doing or using, to clarify something for your own students if it's also unclear to the student teacher, or to tweak other habits or routines that may need it. Modeling reflective practice for the rookies will convince them of its value and get you back in your own groove if need be.

It's a great feeling when you bump into one of them at a conference, too!

Newspaper Coverage

"Any publicity is good publicity," they say. Not so for teachers. Any publicity you receive had better be good, because it reflects on all of us.

Think about it. If a teacher is accused of a crime, the job description always makes it into the headline: "Teacher Accused of Rape", "Teacher Kills Two in DWI Crash", or "Teacher Booked on Assault Charge".

You'll never read "Forklift Operator Accused of Rape", "Electrician Arrested for Domestic Abuse", or "Pastry Chef Booked in Bar Fight".

There are a few professions in whose good company we find ourselves: police, firefighters, clergy, and judges to name a few. All can be called professions of public trust. All are professionals by whom the public feels rightly betrayed when a crime is committed, or even suspected. Whoever said, "More is expected of those to whom more has been given" got it right as it applies to these professions, where trust is concerned. We are held to a higher standard than most because the work we do is arguably more noble than most.

When a newspaper article reporting my imminent retirement made the local paper, I was proud because it mentioned several of my personal achievements and was very complimentary in its tone but, because that isn't normally done, a little embarrassed, too. That is, until I got a phone call from Brian M., a personal friend who teaches in a neighboring district. He'd seen the article and called to congratulate me. I thanked him and said that while I did enjoy the article, it was a tad embarrassing to be praised so publicly.

"Listen, don't be embarrassed. It was great," he said. "Think about the good that it's doing for all the teachers in the area. So often, the paper paints us all negatively because of the bad behavior of a few. It's guilt by association. We get slammed all the time. We don't get the respect we used to. That article will make anyone who reads it think more highly of all of us. You should feel proud."

I do. I feel what more of us should feel, what every teacher ought to feel.

Pride by association.

Graduation ‘76:
scared stiff, but worth every minute.

Afterword

July 20, 2009

Forty years ago today Neil Armstrong and Buzz Aldrin, after a 240,000-mile journey, parked their lunar module on the moon and stepped down onto its surface, becoming the first humans to do so and energizing not only our space exploration program but millions of Americans as well.

This morning, after a 24-mile commute, I parked my car in the lot at the Hamilton-Fulton-Montgomery County BOCES, stepped through the lobby and began the summer curriculum work that I hope will energize not only my teaching career but the nascent careers of the high school seniors who elect the *Careers in Education* program which I have accepted an offer to join in the fall as an instructor. Might as well put all that experience to good use.

It's a beautiful facility with, I'm told, a friendly staff and great kids in the program. Though I have every confidence that it's all true, it will not be the same. I'm sure that it's going to take some time to get used to, and a lot of adjusting on my part.

"One giant leap," indeed.

Appendices

"You were hired to impact lives. You were hired not so much to teach third grade, or history, or physical education, as to influence lives."

- Harry K. Wong

Appendix A

Retirement Remarks by Robyn Thorpe Posson

...Special events like this evening offer opportunities to extol the honoree's many virtues. The one quality I choose to address is the power and scope of Pepe's (for that's what we called him) influence on our class as a whole and on me in particular.

Pepe was, as a fresh-faced new hire in 1972, strong-armed by then-principal George Corrigan to be the advisor for the incoming freshman class. And while he wasn't given much guidance or training in what being a class advisor entailed, I can attest that he hit the ground running.

Pepe has had a long-standing, overarching positive influence on our class. From the get-go, he's been a strong, fair and compassionate leader. He took on the gargantuan task of creating an environment where two hundred twenty-five unique adolescents eventually became a cohesive team, helping us find the threads that held us together and working collaboratively on common goals. Pepe made it known that every class member had a voice and a valid opinion. He treated all with kindness, respect and camaraderie regardless of our place in the high school social strata, and expected that we treat each other in kind. He never spoke ill of anyone, and I can't ever recall him raising his voice in anger. He encouraged teamwork, taught us how to make and respect decisions based on consensus, and to value every individual's input. And as team dynamics go, problems inevitably arose from time to time, but he guided us toward finding the best win-win solutions possible.

Although I'm sure some of his co-workers felt differently about having extra duties and responsibilities piled onto their already-packed teaching schedules, Pepe often spoke about how much he enjoyed being our advisor. He never complained about the countless hours he spent of his own time making everything work, and promised our class that since it had been such a great experience, he'd never take on another class advisor position, and he never did. And we love him for that.

Not surprisingly, as a result our respect and affection for him have continually grown in the thirty-three years since graduation. He's been present for many classmates' weddings and birthdays, has shown unflappable support at funerals, and with his wife Elisa is our guest of honor at class reunions. He was, and remains to this day, a compassionate, open-minded and valued mentor.

We certainly can all agree that adolescence is a time of life where everything is changing – uncertain, sometimes angst-ridden and tumultuous. Pepe was a rock-solid constant in that maelstrom. He had an even-keeled, upbeat presence and a great sense of humor that set a positive tone to my high school experience.

Like most adolescents, I often compared myself to my peers, often feeling inconsequential and invisible. I knew that I fell short on the popularity scale. Every morning before homeroom I'd pop into Pepe's room, where there was always a group of kids gathered. It was there that he consistently recruited us to be active members of our class, and to get involved in the planning and execution of the many activities that we held...

I followed Pepe's advice and enjoyed being an active part of the larger group, but preferred doing the behind-the-scenes work because staying on the periphery was where I felt most comfortable, and I didn't seek or expect anyone to notice my contributions for fear of having any attention pointed my way. But the entry that Pepe wrote in my senior yearbook changed all of that for me. He wrote, and I quote:

> Robyn,
>
> Thank you, thank you for all your time and effort on behalf of my number one love and obsession, the Class of '76. Lots of kids do a great deal and are never recognized for it, and that is where you fall. I want to make sure that you know that I have known all along, and won't ever forget it. Ever. Success and happiness to you always!
>
> Love,
>
> RSP

Now, while those words may initially seem benign and commonplace, as yearbook sentiments stereotypically are, they made a profound impact on me and still do to this day. Many people don't realize that the power of taking just two minutes of time to recognize and validate someone can and does have lifelong significance. And I'd wager that Pepe had no idea that he'd had that kind of positive influence on me.

I have grown into a woman confident in her abilities and who no longer is content to stay in the background. I make a point to recognize others and express gratitude for their special gifts, because I know first-hand the power of telling someone that who they are and what they do matters. Pepe's enthusiasm for the written word sparked a similar interest in me. I earned an undergraduate degree in English, and am writing my first book. Clearly, this student still learns from the teacher.

Pepe, I speak for our entire class when I say that there aren't enough ways to express our sincerest and most heartfelt gratitude for making those sometimes difficult high school years bearable; for demonstrating how walking in integrity and taking the high road is always the best option; and for your kindness, leadership, wisdom and friendship. Enjoy the next chapter of your life, Ace. We love you.

Appendix B

Retirement Remarks by Mark Garwacki

...Here's the cool thing. I was fourteen years old when I met Rick...and now Mr. Pepe is retiring. Where have the years gone? It really does seem like only yesterday that I was a fourteen-year-old kid who walked into his English class to meet his new English teacher.

So, I walk into the room, I look around, I see this slightly older, slightly taller kid with long sideburns and these cool Clark Kent glasses, and I realize that that turns out to be my teacher, Mr. Pepe. You know, back in 1972 Rick was all of twenty-two years old and it wasn't until many, many years later that I realized how much I truly did learn from that twenty-two-year-old kid. I'm very convinced that the very best teachers are those people who teach you something when you don't know you're being taught, and Rick is one of those people. He is truly one of those exceptional teachers.

Over the course of my personal business career I've had the opportunity to work side-by-side with corporate CEOs and company presidents. I've been to dozens of seminars on leadership and on management. And do you know something? None of those high-powered CEOs or any of those highly-skilled and highly-trained seminar leaders taught me anything that that twenty-two-year-old kid didn't teach me back in 1972.

And what he taught me is this: if you want to lead and influence people, the first thing you need to do is to build trust. And in order to build trust, you need to form a bond. Rick formed that bond, and the way he formed that bond is just by being who he is. He was himself from day one, from "Captain Kirk" talking into his wallet...that was him, he never made any bones about it. I think that was the connection. That was why we enjoyed being in his class.

Prior to meeting Rick I never thought – and I'm going to have to apologize to any teachers in this room whose class I was in prior to Rick's, because I'm about to insult you, so get ready – I'd never considered any teacher to be a friend. After all, they were my teachers, and there was that line that you would never cross. But Rick was different. He was my teacher; he was my friend. He was fun to be around, and he made me want to learn. It may sound a little bit corny but I always felt that if I did not do well in his class, that I somehow would be letting him down personally. And I have to tell you, not wanting to let someone down is a sentiment that I only reserved for my parents. So Rick, from my standpoint you're in some pretty good company.

That having been said, I want to leave you with this one final thought: I am sure that on retirement day people tend to get very, very introspective about it. They wonder if their careers had any value or made any difference. Let me take this opportunity personally, on behalf of our entire class, to say that you made a difference. You made a very big difference.

You know, at the end of a lot of careers you have certain things to show for it. Being a teacher, it's not as concrete. If you're an architect, for instance, you have buildings with your name on them that are out there, and you can say,

"Wow, I built that." But you know, Rick – Mr. Pepe – there are thousands of students out there with your name on them. And all of those people are better people for having had the opportunity to call you teacher, and call you friend. And I consider myself extremely fortunate to be one of those individuals. God bless you, Ace.

Appendix C

Retirement Remarks by Shari Rosato Lontrato

I don't have a lot of eloquent things to say to everybody in the room. I just want to speak to you directly.

I first met you twenty-seven years ago when I was a sophomore and walked into your English class. I was not a softball player or a basketball player or on any of the teams that you coached or advised. I was just a student in your class for one year yet, for the last twenty-seven years, whenever I've seen you anywhere in the community or anywhere else, you remember my name. You know exactly who I am and you ask how I'm doing.

That's the kind of impact that you have on students every single day. And there are a lot of students out there just like me, that were just students in your class, walking around thanking you for giving us the confidence and making us feel as though we were important people. So, I just wanted to say to you publicly: Thank you for everything you gave to me, and congratulations on your retirement.

Appendix D

Retirement Remarks by Steven Tommasone

When I got here, everything was fine. I wasn't emotional, but after Robyn, Mark and Shari, I'm feeling a bit of emotion.

Being a student of Mr. Pepe was a wonderful experience. And to tell you what an impact he had, I have to do something here, but I'll keep talking (takes out cellphone)... I can do many things at once because I'm a politician!

Do you remember this? (Music plays.) I'm a big KISS fan too, and he's the reason for it. Just to give you a little personal story...being from a conservative, traditional Italian family, I couldn't play this music very loud in the house.

So, my mother heard this music and saw the album covers and wasn't too happy. But I told her, "Mr. Pepe's an Italian! He's from Amsterdam!" And that made it OK.

Shari and Robyn, you did a wonderful job and I share your sentiments one hundred percent. What I'm here to do briefly is to give Mr. Pepe a proclamation from the town. I also spoke with Assemblyman Amedore and Senator Farley and they've issued proclamations for his many years of service to the community. And I'm going to try to read these without getting emotional because, in your life, you have your parents and people who are good to you...and as a young student, Mr. Pepe was one of the best influences in my life.

About the Author

Rick Pepe taught English at Schalmont High School in Rotterdam, N.Y. for thirty-seven years, and is currently in his third year teaching high school seniors about the profession at the Hamilton-Fulton-Montgomery County BOCES in Johnstown, N.Y. He also coached girls basketball and softball for fifty-two total seasons, advised the Student Council for twenty years, and was advisor to the Class of 1976.

He lives with his wife and inspiration Elisa in Princetown, N.Y.